D0926461

"Jane takes you on the ride of her life, weaving, in emotional detail, the search for her birth family, the shocking circumstances surrounding her adoption, and the dark secrets as deep as the small southern town where it all began. Through thoughtful investigative work, she effortlessly puts the reader front and center as this real-life story of deceit, trauma, and ultimately redemption unfolds. Regardless of our start in life, Jane reminds us, we all have the ability to find humanity if we know where to look."

Lisa Joyner, host of *Long Lost Family*, *Taken at Birth*, and *Find My Family*; adoptee/adoptive mom

"In this gripping story that unfolds like a puzzle with no lid to provide the finished picture, Jane Blasio encounters numerous questions and too many missing pieces of information regarding her origins. Jane's search for answers, meaning, and belonging will take the reader to the darkest places in the human soul, ultimately unveiling the hardest truths to bear and then revealing the beauty found among the scattered pieces of the puzzle."

Anna LeBaron, author of *The Polygamist's Daughter*

"People like to say it takes a lot of courage to do a book like this: I think it takes a sight more than that. Jane Blasio lived a story that most of us could only imagine—from being sold as an infant by a small-town doctor to years of searching for her birth mother. A gut-wrenching ordeal. But she not only lived it, she wrote about it, bringing it all to life for the reader as it poured out of her. Sometimes you have to remind yourself that this was a life lived, not one just crafted."

Rick Bragg, Pulitzer Prize–winning writer, journalist, and author of two bestselling memoirs, *All Over but the Shoutin'* and *Ava's Man*

TAKEN AT BIRTH

TAKEN AT BIRTH

Stolen Babies, Hidden Lies,
and My Journey to Finding Home

JANE BLASIO

Revell
a division of Baker Publishing Group
Grand Rapids, Michigan

© 2021 by Jane Estelle Blasio

Published by Revell
a division of Baker Publishing Group
PO Box 6287, Grand Rapids, MI 49516-6287
www.revellbooks.com

Printed in the United States of America

Library of Congress Cataloging-in-Publication Data
Names: Blasio, Jane, 1964– author.
Title: Taken at birth : stolen babies, hidden lies, and my journey to finding home / Jane Blasio.
Description: Grand Rapids, Michigan : Revell, a division of Baker Publishing Group, [2021]
Identifiers: LCCN 2020049262 (print) | LCCN 2020049263 (ebook) | ISBN 9780800739416 (cloth) | ISBN 9781493430574 (ebook)
Subjects: LCSH: Blasio, Jane, 1964– | Adoption—Corrupt practices. | Wrongful adoption. | Birthparents. | Missing children.
Classification: LCC HV874.82.B58 A3 2021 (print) | LCC HV874.82.B58 (ebook) | DDC 362.82/98092aB—dc23
LC record available at https://lccn.loc.gov/2020049262
LC ebook record available at https://lccn.loc.gov/2020049263

21   22   23   24   25   26   27   7   6   5   4   3   2   1

To Joan, Kitty, and Carlynn
for being who they were and
teaching me about love.

———

Thank you, Rick Bragg,
for giving your support
and telling me years ago
I could tell this story.

CONTENTS

Introduction

I'VE HEARD IT SAID that the devil is in the details. I never thought my life was very different from anyone else's until I began searching for my birth family. What should have been a simple process to access my adoption records became a lifelong quest for truth. A quest riddled with too many details and the devil was definitely in them. My name is Jane Blasio, and I was sold as a newborn in January of 1965 by a doctor in the small North Georgia town of McCaysville.

A factory worker and his barren wife made the journey south to Georgia from their home in Ohio because they had heard they could get a healthy baby from the town's beloved physician, Thomas Jugarthy Hicks, the man who sold me. They kept the car running as Hicks passed me through the back door of his clinic.

The heartbreaking thing is that I wasn't even special. Starting in the forties and lasting over a span of almost thirty years, Doc Hicks built a lucrative business selling babies out of his clinic. In the small town, women had few options and would go to the doctor for help. Some gave their babies freely to him with his promise to find homes and a better life for their children. But others were local housewives who were simply told by Doc Hicks that their babies had died; then he sold them to willing couples with the good fortune to afford them.

The twin cities of McCaysville, Georgia, and Copperhill, Tennessee, share most of everything except zip codes. The painted state line across the blacktop of the grocery store parking lot being the only way to distinguish between the two. Walk with me and see glimpses of the townsfolk, some who, even to this day, believe that Doc Hicks was a godsend—a man who healed both family and friends. Meet churchgoing people and bootleggers alike who feared the doctor and yet did business with him.

You will see the two main characters' lives touch briefly as they move through time and come back together in the search for truth. The two main characters being the doctor who sold me and myself as I grew up always second best, always sitting in the laps of strangers. I'll show you the struggle to understand how flesh and circumstance could be brokered so easily. Cash for a baby and a fake birth certificate.

Let me take you on my personal search that spanned over thirty years, and I will show you, with all the care I can give, the women who lost their babies through the back door of the Hicks Clinic. Let me pull back the veil to show you the many lives touched by both darkness and light. Let me take you through time to the quiet town of McCaysville, to the small brick building of the Hicks Clinic, and introduce you to a baby seller.*

---

* The stories you're about to read are retold as I envision them, having heard the accounts by those who were personally affected. So many were hurt by their experiences at the Hicks Clinic. I've disguised details here to protect their privacy.

ONE

Stolen Babies

I THANK GOD for tattletales. If someone hadn't gossiped like an old hen and let the truth out, no one would have ever known I was someone else's child. My father was clear that he never intended on telling my sister, Michelle, and me that we were adopted, much less that we'd been bought from a clinic best known for abortions. When I first began asking questions, he lied, and when I was older, he admitted that he saw no reason to tell us the truth. My parents knew what they had gotten into when they bought two babies, and everything was, in their eyes, best buried deep somewhere. What a way to live, fearing every day that someone would show up at the house and take us from the front yard. Fear and shame are consequences of keeping secrets, especially when you have so much to lose when they can't be contained.

My father was angry at the person who told his secret. My mother kept quiet because she was afraid. My parents wanted a baby desperately, and they had heard from my mother's aunt Alice that they could get a baby for cash in North Georgia. Aunt

Alice's friend knew a doctor who was selling babies, and they made their way down there to get one.

Nestled in the Blue Ridge Mountains, the Hicks Clinic, which looks today like it did then, is a small, square, brick building the color of homemade butter pecan ice cream, the good kind. The simple, clean architectural lines of the building don't hint at what took place inside. It sits just a stone's throw away from the mild and soft-flowing Toccoa River that snakes its way quietly around McCaysville, Georgia, going deeper into Tennessee and becoming treacherous as it weaves through falls and rough rocks. Just a couple miles downstream, it transforms into the mighty Ocoee River, which is known for its whitewater rapids. The front of the Hicks Clinic faces one of the two main roads into the town, just across the street and down a-ways from the IGA store that straddles the Tennessee and Georgia line. If you were in the courtyard of the Hicks Clinic, you could watch the trains pass behind the IGA parking lot.

Doctor Thomas Jugarthy Hicks planted his building in the heart of McCaysville like you would plant a garden: methodically, one step at a time. The original Hicks Clinic was a house around which he placed offices and examination rooms. When the new clinic was built, the original structure was torn down. In old photos, nothing hints that the original building housed a medical facility or doctor's office. The old structure stood in what's now the courtyard of the Hicks Clinic.

Hicks tended the locals, mostly poor copper miners and their families, for colds, flu, and everyday medical mishaps, but he made his name and wealth through abortions and the sale of babies. He built his practice around the missteps of his life.

In the early 1940s Hicks was arrested and went to prison for selling drugs to the local miners and then lost his medical license and was barred from practicing in Tennessee. But after his release, the people of Georgia took him in and looked the other way long enough for him to open for business in McCaysville.

Hicks was a businessman first. That has never been questioned by anyone who knew him or knew of his practices—local families, workers from the copper mine, young girls seeking help, men needing a forged birth certificate to avoid or get into a war, and those who had to turn to him because they were unable to make it to a hospital. Patients could pay for his services by cash, check, or bartering, depending upon their economic status or inconvenient situation. Hicks's reach included catering to the debutantes from Atlanta. He was the town doctor, abortionist, and baby seller. With prices ranging from one hundred dollars per baby in the 1940s to one thousand dollars per baby by the 1960s, Hicks sold newborns to barren couples from up North who were looking for babies to call their own.

My adoptive father didn't want anyone to know about the Hicks Clinic or the long drives to McCaysville that he and my mother took to buy my sister and me. He especially didn't want others to know about the doctor who was selling babies or the steady stream of women who ended up at the clinic to use the doctor's services for many things my father most assuredly couldn't speak of. The details of what went on at the clinic would be too much for many of our family members and friends. How do you explain buying a baby?

I was around fourteen years old when I saw my birth certificate for the first time. I studied it like an old-world map and used it to launch into many dreams of my birth story. I began piecing together my connection to the Hicks Clinic when I first laid eyes on the document, but my journey started years before on a crisp fall afternoon in Ohio. My first clear memory as a child was when I was told I had been adopted. It was late 1971. I was six years old. Radio stations played James Taylor and Janis Joplin, and President Nixon appeared on the television news. It was a perfect afternoon to play in the backyard.

Fall 1971

The warmth of the sun and the smell of leaves and dirt filled the afternoon air as I played with friends in our backyard. My sister came out to the back porch and called me to come inside. Michelle was ten years old to my six. Answering her as I dug my sneakers into the grass, I checked out my torn jeans. I'd be in trouble when Mom noticed. As I entered through the back door, expecting sweet smells of dinner and finding an empty table, confusion moved me across the room. It wasn't until I passed through the kitchen that I saw the three of them in the living room, silent and scared.

Cigarette smoke filled the room, swirling upward to the ceiling and clinging to its surface. Sunlight filtered in from the kitchen and lit the corner of the living room where my parents were sitting on the sofa. The air was thick with tension, the tightness alarming. It put my guard up and burned the memory into me. Taking it in, I stopped abruptly, then slowly moved closer to stand before them. Jim and Joan Walters didn't look like they were ready to share their news.

My father mumbled as he looked to the floor, speaking just under his breath. I could barely hear him. "We have something to tell you, and it may be hard for you to understand." It was difficult to see him clearly, as he slumped just beyond the shaft of light coming from the kitchen. Cigarette smoke wrapped around his face as he brought his cupped hand to his mouth for another drag. Again silence.

The tension intensified and he finally raised his head without making eye contact, speaking toward Michelle, though not to her, even as she stood directly in front of him. "You heard from the kids on the playground that you were adopted?"

Immediately and through tears Michelle broke open, half screaming from the confusion of what she already knew and the fear of what she was about to be told. "Yes. They said I was a black-market baby too! They said you bought us!"

Even at my young age, I sensed that my father was embarrassed for the intrusion into his private dealings. He could say little more, dumbfounded that it would be so easy to unravel his well-laid plans. My mother's family had always thought the transaction was suspicious, but they had never promised to share in keeping the secret. My father never wanted us to know.

My mother shook off the tension of the moment. Looking between both of us, she spoke with control and little emotion, opening the conversation. "You two were adopted. Do you know what that means?"

Innocent wonder made me look over to Michelle for a hint of what to do. She was my big sister and should've known how to react in that moment. I looked and looked until I realized she wasn't looking my way. She had her head down, and she was crying. I was on my own. My mother turned her attention to me, irritation showing on her face. "How about you?"

I didn't understand the tears or the drama, and I was okay with that, ready to escape. Half asking, half pleading, I jerked out a reply. "Can I go back outside?"

Relieved, she nodded, and I left them fast behind, busting open the screen door. The late afternoon air was a relief from the heaviness of the scene inside. The swing set beckoned me, and I sank into the faux leather of one of the seats, barely shaking the chains that attached it to its metal frame. I forgot about my friends playing out back as the sun was still bright but setting fast. All I can remember is how scared I felt. I'm not sure why; I just was.

My aunt Darlene came around the driveway side of the house, saw me in the yard, and came up to where I was sitting. She didn't know what she was walking into when she stopped by the house. She was my dad's sister, but she was ten years younger than him and was always looking out for Michelle and me. She would detangle my long hair ever so softly, make us peanut butter and jelly sandwiches with our favorite strawberry jam, and make sure we had a good time no matter what we were doing. She was close with and loyal to my parents and lived just down the street from us with Uncle Robby and Cousin Robin in the house Grandpa Walters built.

"What is a black market, Aunt Darlene?" I said, peering up at her through my crazy-cut bangs. She looked nervous, and that was odd, especially since she'd never looked anything but confident and mostly defiant. She took a breath, and I could tell she was thinking.

"Well, that's a question, all right. Ask your dad." She hesitated a moment, then added, "But not today, monkey. Wait awhile."

I never asked him. It all seemed like too much to ask about. And who was I? My aunt didn't bring it up with my parents until I was much older. I'm sure she was waved off and told to stay out of it. My parents had been caught red-handed and didn't want any further talk. They didn't realize their secrecy fueled my interest and a fire began burning, bringing to life in me a desire to know what it all meant for a six-year-old to be adopted and *black market*.

From that point forward the whispers became more evident to me; I heard more of the chatter. Almost wolflike senses appeared when I heard my parents whisper whenever anyone would say Michelle or I looked like them. Or more frequently, when my grandpa talked about how we were different or special. I began noticing how adult relatives smiled hard at Michelle and me every time we walked into the room, as if the uncomfortable grins would hide the elephant sitting in the corner holding a fake birth certificate.

Cousins would make remarks about us being made differently than they were. We were a special delivery of sorts. The neighbors had heard the stories and would share sad looks as my mother and father kept us in the backyard. My mother would all but have a breakdown if we strayed into the front yard or if a car rolled by too slowly out front, fearing someone would come to take us back. I remember the funny looks and comments from the kids at school who, themselves, didn't completely understand why we were different in everyone's eyes. Kids can be cruel and easily pick up on and react to the slightest tension or uncertainty.

Even if someone dared bring up the mystery surrounding my sister and me, how could you explain black-market babies to the third graders at Bettes Elementary School?

Spring 1974

The clock on the wall of the teachers' lounge was ticking too loudly and too slowly. I wanted to go home, to hide. The third grade was not a place of refuge. Not for me. Not on this day or too many others that came after. The large, very blonde teacher on recess duty had brought me in and seated me in the teachers' lounge to get me away from the other children. Three Dog Night blasted from the radio about Jeremiah the Bullfrog but I could still hear the teacher's polyester pantsuit rustling as she hovered mountainous above me with a worried brow and pursed lips. She had found me huddled under a bush on the playground while the other kids laughed and kicked dirt my way.

A cousin of mine had overheard an adult conversation about my adoption. That day I absorbed some of the meaning of *black market* as she matter-of-factly told my classmates that I was paid for in cash like a dog at the store. "A puppy in the window. That's what she is with her new outfit and pretty braided hair. Just a little dog with a new collar." I was wide-eyed with the meanness of it all.

I vividly recall seeing my new red corduroy pants covered with dirt as I looked down at the ground and the children snickering, taunting, and pushing me to tears and confusion with words that I had never thought about or dreamt could be applied to me. As they continued their verbal assault, I stepped back and fell to the ground, kicking up a mess around me. There I sat under the dirt and leaves, now like the very dog I was accused of being, cowering from the blows. But I wasn't a dog. I knew I was adopted but not that I had been bought.

I know now that I was too young to fathom the depth of it. Back then, nobody told me it was okay to ask or wonder about what was being said. They weren't sure what to say to me since I was a child. And I wasn't their child, so it was risky territory for an outsider or anyone wanting to stay in my parents' circle of friends or relatives. The teacher had brought me inside to shield me from the children's cruelty. She smiled a lot and did some low-level doting, wiping my hands and face off and attempting to clean my new outfit enough to look as normal as possible. I'm pretty sure she knew who I was and had heard the circumstances of my "adoption." It was a close-knit neighborhood, and everyone knew who hung what on the line on laundry day. The story most assuredly got around way before I showed up on the playground that day.

I bolted out of the chair and ran when she told me I could go, never once looking up as my classmates moved out of the building as the bell rang for everyone to go home. I wanted to get away. Away from the big blonde hair and the sounds of barking that played over and over in my head. Embarrassment, confusion, and fear moved my legs and arms, propelling me away from the school and toward my house as fast as I could go. Running away from the children and their taunts that were stuck in my mind from earlier and were now a part of my lessons in trust and discernment.

These early lessons became the cornerstone of my fear of never finding the truth. They pushed me as I grew older. I began looking in every dark place, grasping at the tiny pieces of the puzzle I'd glimpsed that day on the playground. I collected everything and anything I could from an offhanded remark, a hushed conversation from my parents or grandparents, a torn page in the family Bible, or an odd number in my mother's contact book. I kept my guard up like a lookout at a bank heist and romanticized the escape. I had to know. The search was on in my very young mind, and although I still wasn't sure what I was looking for, I knew I had to find something, anything, to explain *black market*. On a cold, snowy break from school, my first attempt at direct-line questioning was merely the natural progression of my search.

Winter 1976

Snow covered everything, and at first, it brought the delight of afternoons playing outside, half-buried as we made snowballs and forts with the neighborhood kids and ran around pumped with adrenaline until we couldn't feel our fingers or toes. We'd retreat into the warmth of home, only to thaw out and prepare to do it again once given the go-ahead. Snow. Thaw. Repeat. That's a lot of work for a twelve-year-old.

School had been canceled for the third day in a row because of the onslaught of lake-effect snow coming in across Lake Erie with a vindictive streak, trickling down all the way from Cleveland to Akron. In the 1970s Akron public schools never canceled classes because of snow, so this was a rarity. But by day three I was bored and agitated from sitting around so long.

Having already exhausted almost every opportunity for entertainment outdoors, I decided it was time to explore the house. Curiosity overrode my sense of propriety and drove me upstairs to my parents' bedroom to look for any forbidden thing lurking there. After rummaging through the closet and under the bed and finding little of interest, the dresser was next. Opening the top drawer and making a quick glance back to check that I was still alone, I gingerly touched each stack of my mother's lingerie, fumbling over the softness to see if anything was hidden beneath. Nothing. I went to the next two drawers and repeated the same action, finding only souvenir stamps and silver dollars, leaving me to put all hope into the last drawer.

Finally, the dresser gave up its bounty. Under the thickness of sweaters and scarves, I found what at first glance looked like a scrapbook. I pulled it out and carried it to the table next to the bed. My mind reeled in anticipation as I slung my tiny frame across the mattress, grabbed the book, and settled in for the shameless invasion of privacy. I ran my fingers over the smoothness of the worn, pink quilted satin on the outside of the book and meticulously wound my way to the inside of the front cover. The cream-colored pages were decorated with hand-painted clouds in taupe and blue that floated among images of rattles and storks. The clouds were the backdrop to vital statistics that had been penned by a human hand.

Losing myself in numbers representing the weights and lengths of two babies, the book fell from my grip. It landed in an awkward position, the paper bending against the wood floor. I looked down from the bed but didn't touch it. Instead, I stretched as far as I could over the side without falling, placing my fingers flat against the cover to keep steady as I studied the clouds on the folded, open page.

Two dates were written on the paper, September 20 and January 15. I recognized the first as my sister's birthday, but the second wasn't mine. And when that fact paired with the familiar writing of my mother, it opened a Pandora's box that exploded in a way I can still feel today. My birth certificate, the only one

I knew of, the one I had scrutinized since I was old enough to read, had December 6 on it. The day we celebrated with cake and the birthday song.

It didn't take long to all but fall from the bed, scoop the book into my arms, and descend the stairs, stumbling my way to the kitchen table where my mother sat. I shoved every square inch of the pink book in her face, and she blinked hard, amazed at the sixtyish pounds of sheer attitude standing in front of her, demanding answers. Without a hint of mildness, she spoke in a voice louder than her usual. "That was the day we picked you up from the doctor in Georgia. You were born sometime in January. That's all I know. Your father can tell you more if that's what you want."

The tapping of her fingers on the table and her arched eyebrows told me I had pushed enough for one day. She, too, had had enough of me in the house for three straight days without a break. Triumphantly, I turned and walked away, hearing her now-straining voice behind me, "Put the book back where you found it and stay out of my room." I'll always remember the look on her face, the cigarette smoke billowing as she sat in front of the sliding glass doors, focused on me and my next move.

I didn't stay out of her room as I should have, but the book disappeared. I never saw it again.

These fragments of my early childhood started everything, from my questioning and searching for who I was to the moments of my life that influenced and prodded me along to find out who I am. Those experiences made me feel alone and, most of the time, less than. Everyone else seemed to have so much more insight into life and belonging while I struggled to understand. Struggled to fit in.

Most importantly, these were the moments of sheer truth, of what I had been seeking, and sometimes demanding my whole life. Thankfully not all of my childhood memories are mysterious or challenging. But the yearning to know more didn't stop with each new experience. No, the pull toward the truth was stronger and meant so much more with every year and every clue my hands wrapped around as I grew up and learned more about where I was born and the possibilities of who I really am. I thought about it all of the time, and it danced in the back of my mind no matter what turns my life was taking.

All of the questions I had about who I looked like and who I sounded like and where I came from started to add up. Those simple questions slowly evolved into what I wanted to know most. These are my moments, my memories, but there's so much more to this story than just me. This is about the town of McCaysville, the Hicks Clinic, and the women who stepped into that building and came out without their babies. It's about the family I grew up with and the family I wasn't given the chance to grow up with, the family that lost me. It's about all those who were wrapped up in what Doctor Hicks was doing, and above all, it's about all of those seeking truth.

TWO

Elvis Presley Sunday Religion

ELVIS PRESLEY'S VOICE, low and smooth, softly sang the lines of "The Old Rugged Cross." The words were wrapped in heavy, bass undertones and the added ring of church bells for effect. Half-awake, I listened to the church bells ringing and the beauty of Elvis's voice as they somehow entwined with the smell of bacon and pancakes. Both themes of redemption and the scent of tangy goodness combined as they came wafting from the living room and the kitchen and up the stairs to my room, setting my mouth to watering and my lips to smacking. *It must be Sunday*, I thought. Sunday mornings were made for the King of Rock and Roll and for bacon.

At the Walters household, Sunday morning breakfast was the best. The house was filled to the brim with the smells of an American breakfast: bacon or sometimes sausage, eggs, grits, hash browns, and piping hot black coffee as it percolated on the counter. And, of course, gravy and biscuits. Oh, how wonderful they were.

One Sunday, Elvis was still singing about "The Old Rugged Cross" after the sun had been up for a short while, and the sounds of the small city neighborhood pressed in and finally roused me from my bed.

> To the old rugged cross, I will ever be true
> Its shame and reproach gladly bear
> Then He'll call me someday to my home far away
> Where His glory forever I'll share.

The words slowly, rhythmically worked their way into my head as I made my way to the kitchen table with hair askew and sleep still all over my face. As usual, I began with a glass of orange juice and a handful of bacon. I was all smiles as I pushed the hair off my face with greasy hands, leaving a trail across my forehead and cheeks as I prepared for the next bite. My mother was humming along with Elvis and doing well at holding her own. Her voice was low and pretty, and she had a way with keeping time and key.

"So I'll cherish the old rugged cross, till my trophies at last I lay down . . ." She sang and turned to me, stopping long enough to give direction. "Janie, fill your plate and eat up. We have a lot of work to do today." She said that every Sunday and she meant it. Laundry, the floors, the bedsheets, and the bathrooms. She looked around me to the living room. "Where's Michelle?"

With a mouthful of most everything laid out on the table, I attempted to respond. "Umm . . . not sure . . . don't know . . . mmm . . . maybe upstairs?" Then I continued shoving food into my mouth, munching elaborately.

This was also a tried-and-true ritual we went through every Sunday: get Michelle out of bed. She was a teenager who spent most of her weekends listening to music and staying up with her girlfriends until the sun came up, so getting her moving in the morning was always an effort. My father would go to her room and get her down the steps and to the table. It was no small feat. Then we would finish eating and get started on the one day we had together. Barring holidays, we started every Sunday the same way as early as I can remember.

When breakfast was over, we would all start the chores and clean the house until it was time to go to Grandma's. The entire time we were cleaning, we'd listen to the Elvis Presley hymn album *How Great Thou Art*. Over and over the vinyl would spin and play on the turntable. I loved belting out "How Great Thou Art," "His Hand in Mine," and "Peace in the Valley." Even though my voice was less angelic than most, I knew every word of every one of those hymns, and I would sing them Elvis-style, low growl and everything. We could hear the album with its steady thumping from the semismooth, linen-covered speakers in the credenza and even over the loud clanking and humming of the clumsy vacuum and the crescendo of dishes as they were scrubbed, sprayed down with water, and sometimes dropped into the sink. As my mother pushed us onward to domestic bliss with her terse directions and disappointed sighs, I pictured Elvis's snarl and hips a-moving as the windows were polished, the floors swept, and the bathtub scoured and left gleaming. It was a special kind of religion of its own, and in our little world, we embraced it fully.

Since no one in my family went to church, our neighbor Madeleine took pity on my family's status as almost-heathens and often invited us to First Church of the Nazarene. Madeleine was a wonderful, warm spirit who loved everyone she came across.

She looked and sounded like Katharine Hepburn, so it was an easy invitation to accept. Even though my parents would pass on the invite themselves, they allowed me to go every so often, and I'd jump at the opportunity to get dressed up. The First Church of the Nazarene was a place of wonder and awe, and I have the fondest childhood memories from the time I spent there.

I quickly fell in love with the high, sparkling white walls and the beautiful organ with the pipes that seemed to rise almost to the ceiling. The sounds that came from it were equally beautiful, and I would close my eyes and listen like a little bird on a branch getting ready to fly. That church brought me my first glimpses of praying and preaching, ladies crying and singing, and men all dignified in their suits and hats. I learned how to be still with just the exception of a giggle or two, swaying with the music from one foot to the other. I felt soothed. I'd go to Sunday school on those days, and that's where I first heard of Jesus. They told me to hide Him close in my heart. They also told me how He had died for me and how much He loved me. There were pictures of the cross and men in multicolored robes, fish and loaves of bread, and a boat on a lake. The pictures hung on the painted walls of the basement rooms where we played games that taught us the stories of the Bible. We sang songs and ate cupcakes and cookies. I remember thinking, *This must be what heaven is like . . .*

The love I felt there and the security it gave me in the years to come would prove vital as my world began to creak and shake as my parents began to sink like a doomed ship. Any security I had as a child would soon be gone due to my mother's mental health and my father's diabetes, which tore at both his body and mind.

We carried on with our Elvis Presley Sunday Religion for years, my parents never attempting to go into a church. My father was a self-professing atheist, and my mother didn't think she was worthy of stepping foot into a church. She had been branded by her own conscience after a few missteps in life and deemed herself unworthy.

The 1950s were a lighthearted and wholesome time to grow up but a tough one for a girl pregnant before marriage. My mother knew what everyone thought of a real-life Rizzo right out of *Grease*. She was a tight-sweater-and-high-heel-wearing looker who didn't hesitate to have fun. She was also a rough-and-tumble girl who played softball throughout high school and sometimes got along as one of the guys. When she found out she was pregnant her senior year, she grudgingly went ahead and married her high school sweetheart, thinking she had no other choice. Her heart broke into bits when her baby boy died three days after she delivered him. It was a hard, painful breech birth and the labor and presumed malpractice mangled her body, making it impossible for her to have more babies. Somehow, she saw that as God's punishment.

Her first marriage quickly and violently fell apart after the baby died, and she met my father soon after it ended. Against her parents' warnings, my mother eloped with my father on Thanksgiving Day 1956. They immediately set up house and tried to adopt a baby from the Summit County Children's Services, but it was to no avail. They didn't have enough money in the bank, and my mother had been divorced. Both were big no-no's for adopting. And they wanted a newborn baby, not a three- or four-year-old. For whatever reason, they became picky, and their chances of adopting through legal channels dropped.

It wasn't long before they followed the same path to Mc-Caysville as my mother's aunt Alice to buy Michelle from the Hicks Clinic and returned four years later to buy me. They simply contacted Doctor Hicks and asked to be added to a list of couples who wanted a baby and then waited for a call to pick one up.

My mother soon found out there was condemnation in that as well by overhearing the stories told behind her back of barrenness and stolen babies. The looks and whispers were too much to ignore. She felt more condemnation than anyone should, and it showed in the mental health challenges she faced, including attempting to take her life about every six or eight months from the time I was eleven until I was seventeen.

After each attempt, my father would sit Michelle and me down and tell us we must be better for her. Surely it was our fault she was broken. The three of us were to blame, and her burden was rationed out like bitter medicine. We could clean better or be more attentive or more grateful. My mother wasn't a talker, and she was even quieter when it came to me. I can count on one hand how many times I had a long conversation with her about anything. Mostly it was short quips of direction or comments on how disappointing the day had been, and then she would fall asleep watching television. I was sure her suicidal tendencies were just another reason for me to be considered second best, and the list was long, even at eleven years old. Michelle felt it as well. From the outside, our family may have looked typical, but inside we were broken shards of glass.

I don't know if my mother ever heard my father blame us for contributing to her depression. All I know is she wanted to die right up until the moment she found out her body was consumed with cancer and was told by the doctors that she was going to die. Then she fought like a lion to stay alive and was battling death with every day she faced. The irony was that it was what she had once wished for with all of her heart.

   As I grew older, she knew I wanted to find my birth family and learn more about my birth story, but I didn't have the heart to ask her about it. I didn't want her to think I was replacing her. When we found out she had cancer, any searching I had done already or was working on became an undercover operation. I decided to stick with asking my father for information regarding my birth. My mother had been dying of a broken heart and regret almost her entire life. She battled with falling short of her own expectations, and I didn't want her to think she was falling short of mine. She spent her adult life not knowing she could fly, weighed down with condemnation from the past, clinging to the branches and afraid to take flight. The fight for her life had begun, and at forty-seven, she finally realized she was too young to give up on life.

   Silence surrounded her labored breathing as I sat watching. It had snowed heavily earlier in the evening and now only a few small flakes fell outside the window. The lights in the parking lot gave the snowflakes a shimmering backdrop, outlining the delicate lines of each as they floated downward. The hospital was always too quiet for me, but it was good to see my mother sleeping for more than a few hours at a time. Being there during third shift was the only way I could have one-on-one time with her, and I settled in, even if it was just to watch her rest. She had slept for five hours now. After five years of fighting cancer, my mother had wasted away to a mere eighty pounds on her 5'6" frame, and at fifty-two, she was too young to die. At twenty-two, I was too young to have to watch. That night, like most other nights, she lay childlike in the bed, still and blanketed in. But then the morphine fell short, and she woke in a fit of confusion and pain. I sat in the chair beside her, listening though only half-awake.

Her voice startled me as she began to speak. "I told your father to tell you everything."

It took me a minute to figure out what she was talking about. I looked over at her and nodded in agreement as I took in her words.

"I told him not to lie to you," she continued. "You need to know the truth. It's time to live the truth like you wanted, Janie." Again, I nodded in agreement.

And then, with a shaking voice, she said, "I'm sorry."

I reached out and kissed her forehead as the snow began falling heavier outside the window. The nurse came in and gave her another shot of morphine to ease the pain. Those were her last words to me. I knew then that she understood, had been watching me for all those years. She wanted the best for me, despite never telling me she loved me or showing any affection. But I knew then that she did love me. I closed my eyes and could see her clearly in my mind, singing "The Old Rugged Cross," the tone and rhythms perfect.

All of those years, she knew religion only as Elvis hymns and hadn't known what it was to be forgiven and truly loved. She found redemption with Jesus a month before that night at the hospital, in the last months of her life. Giving her soul to Him completely, she was finally filled with love. From the day she laid it all down, she smiled even through the morphine and pain. For the first time in her life, she was loved no matter what she had done before. She was free from condemnation. The burden was lifted, and she was finally that little bird sitting on a branch waiting to launch and fly high, to glimpse and then reach out to God through song and praise.

THREE

Promise Kept

EVERYONE LOOKS at their life history in segments. Sometimes they're defined by circumstances, like when a parent or whole family goes through challenging times. Or they can be made up of time spent at a favorite house or in a favorite neighborhood. A lot of my segments are connected through my relationship with my father, especially when I was very young and he took me with him everywhere. Although we had our moments, there wasn't always a fight or grudge between us. I idolized him as a child, was his sidekick, and loved the fun he brought to everything. Hanging out at his truck shop like a grease monkey, fixing tires, tinkering with the trucks, and sweeping the floor—I could take in the smell of gasoline and tar all day as if it were Chanel No. 5. He created an independent, strong-willed tomboy and would later regret the mouth that came with it because we never really got along from about the time I was thirteen, even when we both tried real hard.

James William Walters was an attractive and intelligent man who thought he was too smart to lead a normal life. Tall, street-smart, and quick with a comeback no matter what was thrown his way. He earned a degree in computers after an honorable discharge from the United States Air Force. Though he had no guarantee of a bright and prosperous future, he got a good jump on one when he met my mother. He fell for her fast. He was working at First National Bank at the time but grew tired of it quickly and quit on a whim. After a stint at Goodyear, he joined the Akron Police Department. Everything was going well until he was injured during an apprehension and assigned to light duty on the stolen property desk. While there, he either partnered with fellow officers to fence the stolen property or he was the ringleader. I never quite got the whole story.

Over the years I heard the stories from other cops about activities that led to my father serving time. After his first prison spell, he emerged humble and repentant, as he did for each stint for the felonies that followed. Despite these shortcomings, I remember being so proud of him as a child. His uniform was always nice, and he looked so handsome.

The morning they came to arrest him for the first time, I was just nine years old. My mother tried to get me out of the line of sight, but I saw the police coming up the driveway before she pulled me away. My father worked endlessly to start fresh and build a successful long-haul trucking business. But then he'd get caught up in an illegal scheme, and everything he'd worked for would be blown away almost instantly. He'd do his time and start again.

With all of his failings, no one could deny that my father loved my mother with everything he had in his being. He just didn't love her or anyone else enough to keep his nose clean for more than a few years at a time. We watched as his body began breaking down after years of diabetes as his practice of self-regulating it with Reese's Cups and Coca-Cola instead of insulin led to kidney failure and blindness that set in at an early age. One day I came home from high school to find a party at our house. When I asked what was going on, he smiled and my mother laughed as he told me that the doctor who had given him six months to live in 1972 had died that day—it was 1982. He celebrated through a succession of doctors until he passed in 1995, celebrating each time he outlived one.

He and my mother continued their journey together into their last years, and they both knew there wasn't much time left. It was heartbreaking and overwhelming to see them both strive to stay alive. Their last few months together were spent at the hospital, still hoping her cancer would go away.

After my mother's funeral in January of 1988, I spent a few months planning the next step in my search and wondered if my father would honor her wishes by telling me the truth. I'd already spent several years researching and sneaking around with my birth search. Knowing him, I figured he would either tell bigger lies about the Hicks Clinic or tell me everything he knew in great detail.

He was getting sicker by the day, and his mind was closing in on him as well. I knew the chance I was taking by asking anything too deep and was too familiar with his degrading meanness when I did. But I had to try.

The day I decided to talk to my father, my mind wandered to a time in my early teens when I spoke up against him when he was making the same worn-out point about one person being better than others. I worried asking questions would start our feud once again. Memories of the old fight flooded my mind.

"Michelle was pure Georgia stock. But Hicks said he couldn't make us a guarantee about where you came from."

Growing up, that statement was thrown at me whenever he thought I needed to be humbled or had gotten out of line. Little did he know his verbal abuse evolved into my own personal training on what racism looked like and made me more determined to find out about my heritage. I didn't like to be told no, and he was unknowingly, unintentionally molding me for a lifetime of diehard tenacity. I would be very proud to be anything as long as I could know for sure, and I often chuckled as he attempted to insult me that way.

One time, I had had enough. "You paid cash for me," I responded right there at the supper table. He was stymied. I could see it on his face. So I went on without blinking. "You paid for a baby and you have no idea where it came from." That conversation went from zero to sixty in record time, even by the Walters family standards, and I was on the brink of being slapped down.

Closing my eyes to the past, I focused on asking the questions my mother had told him to answer.

A rerun of *Hawaii Five-O* was blasting on the TV in his bedroom, and we sat there talking over the noise about the good days of TV shows like *Baretta* and *Sanford and Son*. We bantered back and forth on who was the best boxer of all time—Jack Dempsey, Muhammad Ali, or newcomer Mike Tyson—until he needed to sit back to rest a little. We silently took in the last of the *Hawaii Five-O* episode as I contemplated how to start the conversation.

"Do you remember telling me about the Hicks Clinic a few years back? About my birth certificate and it being fake?" He sat on the side of the bed, slowly swinging his feet back and forth. He took a deep breath and let it out with a sigh as he looked up at me through the thick-framed, tinted glasses he wore to help with the blindness that was slowly taking over.

"Yes, I do. What else would you like to know? I'll try to remember as much as I can."

And just like that, he became a wealth of information and told me everything without sarcasm and with care and understanding. I took in everything and went back for more and more as he explained what he knew about the Hicks Clinic. He told me how my great-uncle Norm and aunt Alice had bought a boy, my cousin Markie, from Doctor Hicks. He was killed by a passing truck right in front of their house on Blaine Avenue in Akron's North Hill when he was only twelve years old. Aunt Alice knew a woman who had grown up in McCaysville and then moved to Akron to marry her sixth husband. She was the connection to Doctor Hicks and his clinic.

My father changed the subject from Markie to why he and my mother went to the Hicks Clinic and said he knew without a doubt he had made the right decision to take my mother there to get a baby. He had watched her struggle with the desperation to become a mother as her brother and sister started having babies. By the time Michelle was born, my uncle Dickie had two babies with his wife and my aunt Baby had already had three herself. As he recalled these details, I could see the pain on his face from all those years ago.

He talked about the ease with which they made their way down to McCaysville to get Michelle and how the nurse there had put my mother in a hospital gown and placed the newborn in her arms for my father to walk in a little later like she had just given birth. Flowers, pastries, and coffee were there for the mothers and fathers as the clinic was full and vibrant with commotion and hope for the couples buying their babies. He contrasted this account with what happened when they went back to get me.

"When we got Michelle, we told Hicks to keep us on the list for more babies, and we finally got a call. He said I needed to come very quickly for this baby or, well, he meant you. He told us to bring cash this time and to ring him when we were in town, not to go directly to the clinic." My father smirked. "It was a short phone call and when I asked if we could have a boy, Hicks said it was what he had today or nothing. He had others on the list he would call if we didn't want this baby." Amused at the insight, I suddenly understood why I was always allowed to hang out at my dad's garage and be the tomboy, all sneakers and dirty faced.

My heart jumped with every detail as we had our "Hicks conversations," and I sat like I had in my childhood, listening to his every word and emotion. He'd smile talking about how happy they were to get a baby and how much my mother loved dressing us up. He cried many times as he grieved over losing her and shared how much he missed her and the good times. He filled me in on so much, keeping his promise to the love of his life. The most poignant and hard-as-rock memory he shared was his account of what happened when they picked me up.

"We drove into town late afternoon and waited for the doctor to answer the phone. We'd driven all night. It rang and rang until finally someone answered, but it wasn't Hicks. It was a woman, and she told us to pull around to the back of the building close to the door and not get out of the car. We did as directed but didn't know what to think about it since the first time with Michelle was so different." He paused and shut his eyes, trying to bring that time back. I waited quietly, patiently, until he started speaking again.

"We thought we were going to go inside from the back door. But then there he was with a bundled-up blanket. He handed you out to us through the window and took the cash and turned and went back inside. We looked at the bundle and couldn't believe what we were looking at. You were tiny but also covered in dried blood and filth from the birth. Your mom was crying, and we sat there shocked until we heard the door closing abruptly. We left and drove as fast as we could to Akron, stopping only when necessary. We were afraid of being caught with a dead baby."

I sat there with him, trying hard to think through what he'd just said. "A dead baby?"

He looked at me with his head cocked to one side and his eyes rolled as if to say I was stupid, and then he let out a small laugh when he realized I wasn't keeping up. "We didn't think you'd make it to see our doctor, and we couldn't go to a hospital. How would we explain it? No birth certificate, no pregnant mother, no nothing. You were so sickly and a mess. You screamed when we'd touch you, or you were very quiet, too quiet, the other times. We were pretty sure your toes were mangled somehow by the looks of them. And he didn't even give us a receipt. We got a receipt with Michelle." He stopped and thought about that for a moment before continuing.

He shook his head at the whole adventure of going to Mc-Caysville, and I couldn't erase one detail of the story. I couldn't shake it. A receipt. A receipt for a baby. I burned, not at him this time but at the circumstance of a baby and a receipt and the two connected to each other.

After that first breakthrough, there were a hundred conversations with my father about the Hicks Clinic and how they got Michelle and me and why. The last conversation I had with him about everything was wrenching. I had already made plans to visit the clinic before we started talking. My father began telling me about the town of McCaysville as he could remember it and worked his way to what he thought I should do when I got there. Something came up about the birth mothers, and he started to get nervous. He asked if Michelle was in the house and when I had shaken my head no, he started crying but soon it turned to almost wailing. My aunt Darlene came out of the kitchen where she had been cooking dinner to see what was wrong, but my father brushed her away. He had admitted to few things in his life until that day when what started off as another one of our "Hicks conversations" ended with his acknowledgment of what my mother and he had done to Michelle and how he had grieved over it all these years as one of the biggest mistakes he'd ever made.

Michelle tried to hide it from them, but they found out when her clothes could no longer cover her secret. The day they learned about her pregnancy, my father sat with his head down and tears falling from his face as Michelle pleaded with him to let her keep the baby. He could do nothing since my mother had already made up her mind that Michelle wouldn't make the same mistakes she had. So they made a mistake that was far worse than being pregnant out of marriage and devastated their young, vulnerable daughter. They took her to the hospital that day and made her give up the baby she had longed for. Since I could remember, Michelle had wanted to be a mother and wanted her own child. And they took that from her in a violent, horrific manner. At seven months along, she was forced to give birth to her baby in a late-term abortion.

And at that point, that moment, my mother's unworthiness had spilled over to Michelle, and I saw my sister start to struggle with never being good enough. Michelle was never the same after that. Everything she did was tainted by the pain and destruction forced upon her. She crawled through life and fought to survive, thinking she was worthless. Ashamed, she let others treat her like garbage because she didn't think she deserved better. And I hated my parents for it. I hated them at that moment and a million times after for years on end. They had longed for babies but made my sister give hers up, just like the birth mother they got her from. With every drama our family experienced, I drew further into my romanticized dream of my birth family.

Despite all the drama, however, my parents were giving people. They never passed up an opportunity to help those in need. Whether it was a neighbor kid who needed shoes or a coat, they assisted. If a family friend needed a place to stay during bad times, our home was theirs. Several cousins had lived with us over the years for one reason or another and if my mom's friends needed a few bucks to get to the end of the month, they only had to ask. My mother had heard that a teenage neighbor was being physically abused by her stepfather, and she went right over with a Louisville Slugger in hand, got her, brought her to our home, and sheltered her till she was old enough to make her way. Regularly, they'd buy items for friends when they knew they were struggling, stuffed animals for their kids, cigarettes and Coca-Cola in bundles and half gallons of ice cream to lift the clouds off a bad time or two. My parents were always there for friends.

The "Hicks conversations" with my father had given me plenty of material to use for investigating and adventuring from Ohio to Georgia and beyond, and I was ready to leave my childhood, the drama, and anything else behind in order to start fresh in the town of McCaysville.

Years before, when I began searching at eighteen, I contacted a private investigator in New York known for adoption research. After I told him my story, he told me it would cost five hundred dollars a day to hire him with no idea how long it would take because it sounded like an illegal adoption. He asked me what research I had done so far. I outlined my steps to that point, including my research. He took it all in and asked a few more questions before being nice enough to tell me I could do it myself. He suggested I find work with a private investigation firm to hone my skills. Immediately, I found a couple of firms in Akron and started on cases involving workers comp fraud, warrants, surveillance, and basic courthouse research. Slowly I began getting the skills recommended by the New York gumshoe. All the while I had my eyes on McCaysville, waiting for that next step.

FOUR

Long Haul to Georgia

THE HIGHWAYS TO GEORGIA easily moved under my tires that day in 1988 as I sped past the cities and towns going south. I couldn't wait to see the town of McCaysville and wondered if just maybe I'd stumble across someone who looked like me. Interstate 75 was built for quick access to most of the eastern side of Tennessee. The ride down took about ten hours. There were mom-and-pop restaurants and a few antique shops within view of the interstate, but I stopped only when absolutely necessary.

Driving through Tennessee, past Sweetwater, then to Cleveland and Ducktown, following the signs east toward Georgia that took me in and out of the national forest. The route wound through and over the railroad tracks that were bunched together like a nest of snakes right out in front of the Company copper mines. I pushed through the outskirts of Copperhill and headed to the edge of the state of Tennessee. I looked around and took it in with numb confusion. McCaysville was just over the Tennessee line into Georgia, and it was ugly. Ravaged by flooding and neglect, it was dirty and broken—not a comforting sight. I'd like to tell a story of a beautiful entry into my search, the start of the physical quest in the town where I was born, but that would be a lie.

With the information my father had told me about McCaysville, I was not expecting this. I had driven down with a friend and had promised there would be a quaint town and a great time ahead of us. But I stood facing the town and wondered if my friend would ever accompany me on a road trip again. We drove around and looked at the buildings, slowly passing the Hicks Clinic and taking a slight detour around to the back of it, before finding our way to the river that ran through the middle of the town. The Hicks Clinic was only about fifty feet from the Toccoa River, where we stopped. I took it all in, still semistunned. Standing at the river's edge, we watched the water roll and some ducks swimming and feeding. As I expected, my friend was a bit disappointed that there would most likely be nothing to do after dinner. This town had already rolled up its sidewalks by three in the afternoon. We looked around a bit more and decided to head to Atlanta. I had some research to do at the vital statistics building the next day. As we left the town that held so much mystery for me, I made plans to come back to McCaysville on my own later. We drove to Atlanta and found a place to sleep for the night in preparation for the morning of exploring.

My first stop the next morning was the Georgia Bureau of Vital Statistics. I could tell the woman at the counter was busy.

I was sure of it by the way she stood there looking at me above her glasses. Over several years, I had made numerous phone calls and sent multiple letters to the state of Georgia Vital Statistics Bureau in Atlanta to ask about the process of getting access to my A-File, the buried birth certificate that shows the birth mother and father when a legal adoption takes place. Those phone calls gave me a wake-up of sorts. They confirmed what I had overheard as a child and had more recently been told by my father, the facts I suspected all along. My adoption wasn't legal. My calls to them began by asking for the A-File and then slowly shifted to questions about Fannin County and the town of McCaysville.

Going back in my mind to the calls, the nice lady on the phone always tried to understand but fell short each time.

"We don't have a birth certificate for you," the lady would say. "There's nothing here, honey. Try Tennessee. They may have it there."

Then I'd explain about the birth certificate I had in hand again. "But I have a state of Georgia birth certificate with a seal. I can send you a copy of it. How could it be Tennessee?"

"Oh, honey, I'm not sure but sometimes it just turns up that way. Check there." And with that she would be off the phone.

That was how many of the calls went in my attempt to sort out the dilemma of why my state of Georgia birth certificate was somehow not documented. So I contacted the state of Tennessee and they referred me to North Carolina and they sent me to South Carolina. Before I was directed to call more of the fifty states, I stopped the cycle and called the Georgia Vital Statistics Bureau again. Full circle, I was back on the phone, asking the same questions I had on the first few calls. She gave the same responses. My questions remained unanswered, and I knew a visit was needed.

So there I stood at the counter with a stupid smile on my face, ready to ask the same questions. She was still staring at me above her glasses when I introduced myself and explained that I had called several times and was looking for a buried birth certificate. I stopped short of rehashing the whole story when she put her hand up like a ping-pong paddle about to smack down the winning point. My eyes flung wide open and I was close to hitting the floor because now I was worried about getting smacked. I no longer had the stupid smile on my face. And just like that she smiled a big smile and purred. "Oh, you're that baby girl that has a birth certificate but doesn't really. Up north, right?"

I nodded and took a deep breath. Still wary of her paddle hand, watching it and tracking what she was saying and her facial expressions. "Yes, ma'am. Fannin County. McCaysville."

She said nothing, so I continued. "Do you know if there's a buried certificate? I was adopted. My sister too. Michelle Walters. We're both Walters."

She seemed slightly sad when I said that and looked at me for a few minutes before speaking. Her nose crinkled and I could see her battling the pity. "We don't have nothing here for ya. We don't have a thing on you or your sister. Try the courthouse in Blue Ridge. That's the county seat for Fannin. Sometimes they do their own certificates, and we don't see one bit of them."

I had known what she was going to say. I just had to stand there and hear it for myself, no matter how disappointing.

With that, I turned and left the wasted inquiry behind me. It was time to start looking elsewhere. My friend and I spent a few days at the downtown Atlanta Public Library researching newspaper stories and obituaries, gleaning any information we could about Doctor Hicks, his heirs, the town of McCaysville, and the Hicks Clinic. I scrutinized every event that took place in McCaysville, Copperhill, and Blue Ridge. Deaths, births, reports of homecoming queens and sporting events, fires, mining accidents, and even the weather reports were read and assessed for copy worthiness. Any bit of information that would give me insight to find something or someone to help me with my search for my birth family. After spending several days at the library and exhausting the articles on the small towns of McCaysville and Copperhill, I decided to move on to the next step, and my friend and I found ourselves fumbling with a map of Georgia. We set our sights on the Fannin County Courthouse.

Almost three hours after leaving Atlanta, we arrived in Blue Ridge. We had passed right by it on the way from McCaysville to Atlanta but here it was. I was impressed by its simple quaintness. Not stripped bare of beauty by the copper mining industry like McCaysville, Blue Ridge had a distinctly colorful way about it. Everything was very green and lush, and the air smelled of pine. The railroad divided the downtown area, splicing the two main roads. The train stood proudly as the town tourist attraction, displayed in the middle of the Blue Ridge hub, waiting to be fired up and shown off to visitors and townsfolk alike.

The two separate pieces of Main Street, East Main Street and West Main Street, run parallel to each other, right down the middle of Blue Ridge, one sitting lower than the other. When we arrived, people were moving up and down the street and traveling across the railroad tracks to the other side for shopping and business. East Main Street showcased a jewelry shop that housed turquoise and other precious jewels mined from the area and an art gallery that included Cherokee artifacts, mountain cabin furniture, and Bev Doolittle prints of Native Americans, horses, and buffalo blending intensely into the background of forests and high grasses of the Great Plains. A couple antique shops framed the street like old, hand-carved wooden bookends found at a museum. A few houses sat on the sides, but the town was mostly made up of businesses and shops.

On the west side of Main Street was a library and another business at the corner, the business being the cornerstone in a dark brick building with white-cased windows and lettering across them like a scene from *It's a Wonderful Life*. Next to the library stood the Fannin County Courthouse with its grand columns and high steps leading to the double doors. I looked at it with awe. A fine specimen of Southern tradition and legal prowess and, quite possibly, the key to many questions I had.

I walked up those steps as I had walked into the Atlanta Vital Statistics Office. Hopeful. And naive. To this day I can tell you I love those steps; they gave me strength to walk through the doors and into the foyer of the courthouse. Maybe the solid brick and stone beneath my feet gave me the feeling of something so unshakeable that it reminded me I was there for a purpose. The building interior didn't disappoint with its detailed casings and woodwork. The foyer was grand and opened directly into the main courtroom. A turn to the left or right led to several offices and a stairwell. The steps going down were plain in contrast to the ones going up, with richly painted portraits of important politicians or founding citizens of Fannin County lining the walls.

As I looked around that first day, I found a directory on the wall. My work in private investigations taught me that there would be attorneys, staffers, complainants, town reporters, and nosy neighbors mingling nearby. I kept my eyes and ears peeled appropriately. My finger traced the names and numbers.

Probate Court stood out and I knew that was where the birth and death certificates were stored. There was no better place to start than there, so I headed in that direction. I'd romanticized this moment for a long time and felt like this was a first date. My palms were sweaty, and my heart was racing. The sign above the door was clear. It read PROBATE, and I walked in and looked around the small space designated for keeping old records. The office had been reconfigured at least once, by the looks of it. There was the main room, which was very small and fairly dark. Inside was what looked like an old vault door that swung open and was pinned to the wall. Inside the doorway, as I could just see into it by a couple feet and at an off angle, was a wooden island made up of drawers. Stacks of wooden shelves lined the wall that I could see in the very small, vault-like room. Once in the room, I turned in the direction of the voice welcoming me to the office.

With a smile, I approached a woman sitting behind a desk and inquired about birth certificates even though I had my own in hand. She told me the probate judge was busy at the moment, and I asked her when he would return because I had a few questions. She sized me up and asked if she could help, so I showed her my birth certificate and asked if she knew anything about Doctor Hicks. She shook her head and said maybe the judge could help. She chitchatted with me about microfiche and mentioned how a courthouse fire had destroyed most of the old records and she didn't know what they had left. After standing there for a while, I asked where I could find the bathrooms, and she directed me to head around the corner and down the steps to the basement. Not knowing when the judge would return, I took in everything I could, thankful that court was in session and no one was lingering outside the now-closed, wooden courtroom doors.

As I headed around the corner, I heard the voice of the woman in the office trailing behind me. "Don't mind the boxes on the way down. They're temporarily there till we can clean out a spot for them. Just be careful and don't trip. I wouldn't think anything you're looking for would be in there, but you never know for sure these days." Unfortunately, the warning about tripping came too late.

Stumbling down the steps after snagging my foot on a box, my eyes were open about as wide as they could've gone without falling out of my head. I turned and looked at the box. It was a mess and smelled musty and was full of papers and folders mashed together. The cardboard was water-damaged and was very flimsy and deteriorated. I quickly sat down right there and thumbed through a few pieces of paper. But nothing about its organization made sense; it was just thrown together like a salad. Nothing was chronological, numbered, or even marked on the edges of the papers. There was only one common denominator for all: each paper had a header of Fannin County Courthouse across the top and the words *Fannin County* peppered throughout.

I buried myself in the names and circumstances of court cases and public dockets from long ago. I should've been worried about being caught, but I wasn't. This was too interesting, and I needed a clue or two to keep going. The mustiness of the documents made my eyes water and nose run as I sat there hunched over the boxes.

Then as I moved papers around and tried to balance the bottom of the box between my leg and the step as I rummaged through it, my eyes flew quickly to the word *Hicks*. The name jumped at me from the paper that was now resting between my thumb and index finger. I'd heard the probate staff discussing moving some of the older records to the storage room in the basement, something about microfiche and Atlanta making requirements that made no sense for them in the north of the state.

It was almost as if they wanted me to look in those unlidded boxes. They were just open with nothing shielding them from a passerby. Thoughts of stealing a few came to mind and I tried to focus on the document and not make a run for the door with the papers in hand. Names of jurors, case numbers, dates, descriptions of evidence, and the header declaring the state of Georgia against Thomas J. Hicks were all there. Indictment charges. Abortion. Sheriffs. I was reading as fast as I could and realized I had left my notepad on the counter in the probate lobby, leaving me with nothing but a pen to write down all the details.

Voices were still bouncing off the walls and making their way to me, so I panicked and left the boxes before anyone caught sight of what I was doing. Racing to the bathroom to avoid getting kicked out of the courthouse, I stumbled the whole way as I struggled to pull the pen out of my pocket to write what I could across my hand and up my arm. Like tattoos I meticulously wrote what I thought was important.

In many cases of searching for birth, marriage, death, and business records, I've always found it interesting that there always seems to be a courthouse that has burned down or flooded, leaving everyone to guess at details long lost to history. It had only been a little over twenty years after the events that played out at the Fannin County Courthouse to indict and convict Thomas Hicks, and records were disappearing.

But those few moments of discovery on the basement steps made me feel like a character in a fairy tale picking up bread crumbs along the path of where I was supposed to be going, and it made me smile then and it still makes me smile today. By the time I made my way back to the probate office, the judge still hadn't returned, and I thought it would be best to get out before I got myself in trouble. I knew I'd return.

From Blue Ridge, my friend and I headed back through Mc-Caysville on our journey north. For such a small town, there were enough turns for us to take a wrong one. What I thought would take us through Copperhill and into Ducktown, snaked up and around a couple hills until we realized we were lost again. On the winding road with few driveways, a cemetery was ahead on the right and we turned in and took the circular driveway that encompassed the entire layout of headstones and crypts. Close to the cemetery exit, I almost missed something important and would have driven past if the sun hadn't been hitting it just right. A mausoleum with the name *Hicks*. I hit the brakes and we sat there. My eyes locked on the stone building ahead of us until my curiosity held hands with the adrenaline that began running through my veins and I got out to take a look. There the doctor was laid to rest right in front of me. Enamored with the discovery, I made a promise to return to that mausoleum and headed back to McCaysville, finally rolling into Tennessee and down the River Road to Chattanooga for more sleuthing before heading home to Ohio.

This was the first of several trips to Georgia and the small town of my birth, and even if it wasn't the most fruitful attempt at finding more about my birth story, it was a good start. After I got home, I spent time tracking down more information on McCaysville and the surrounding areas from what I could glean at libraries and very early internet forums and chat rooms, but there wasn't much. Looking up information on Doctor Hicks and his family consumed me. I spent hours asking my father questions and piecing his answers together to make some sense of how the Hicks Clinic operated from day to day. Any morsel of information I could find was noted in my journals and tucked away in the back of my mind, categorized for use at a later time when it was relevant. I took stock of where I was in the search and what my next steps would be as I planned my next visit to McCaysville.

Even more important than my plans and next steps, a connection was forming between me and Doctor Hicks, and I couldn't get the cemetery where his mausoleum sat out of my mind. Sitting at the highest point in the cemetery, that mausoleum overlooked the rest of the graves, like one that doesn't want to turn its back on the others. It was placed strategically. Anyone standing next to it and looking north would see the beautiful landscape of rolling hills and high points across from the Ocoee River and into Tennessee. The sight of it haunted me with its serenity and yet its intensity. Sure, there was beauty in the orange clay trailing up the sides of mountains, weaving in and out of what vegetation and small, newly planted pines that were like anchors across the landscape. And the blue sky was bright and vibrant with white clouds floating here and there from that vantage point in the cemetery. It was mesmerizing to me, and I had to go back to see it again. There was so much to find, and everything was calling me to return.

FIVE

Casing McCaysville

IN THE EARLY DAYS of my search, I felt like Indiana Jones each time I got behind the wheel to drive to Georgia. McCaysville was so far away, it was almost always an adventure from the start of the engine. I can't fully describe how it felt to pack a bag and head south, knowing I would soon be back in unknown territory looking for clues. The shadows of the information I already had painted my thoughts the entire drive. Never knowing what to expect was the Indiana Jones part, and getting information out of McCaysville was the treasure.

Making my way back to McCaysville on my second trip, I drove all night and found the road to the cemetery in the predawn light, winding across state lines in, out, and between Tennessee and Georgia to get there. The towns of Copperhill and McCaysville are funny that way. The intermingled roads and boundaries make you question which town you're in at any moment. Returning to where I left off the last trip, I pulled into the cemetery and got out of my car. This landmark had become my point of beginning, and I intended to find what I was looking for.

Oddly and out of the norm, no one was buried in the crypt. The Hicks family was laid to rest next to it like everyone else in the cemetery. The mausoleum became my outpost, my command center of sorts. The sunrise inspired me and set me on my path for each day. I'd lift my voice to God for guidance and protection in the mornings and again in thankfulness in the evenings.

If I close my eyes, I can remember the sights and sounds as the sun began to rise and how the dirt shone like burnt orange stripes across the base of the mountains. I'd heard the stories of the copper mines spewing chemical waste into the air over the last few decades and how it wreaked havoc on the trees, stripping the land bare of its base and leaving little life for the pines. The sights appeared almost watercolored in the morning and gave a dewy, calming start to my day. Sitting in the grass not far from the Hicks family crypt, taking it all in while wrapped in an old quilt picked up at a secondhand store, I thought about what I would do that day, what I would do to find out who I was.

Once I learned Doc Hicks was dead and buried at the cemetery in Copperhill, each of my search days started and ended there, just like the first morning of that second trip.

That morning, like most every other morning of my life, the one thing that motivated me most was my stomach. It was talking to me, so I pulled up stakes at the cemetery and made my way into town to find something to eat. Winding my way through the main street in the two towns was becoming familiar. Thankfully wrong turns were becoming fewer, and I was getting a feel for the route. Driving slowly past the buildings, I saw only two choices for food: a gas station with window signs heralding the finest breakfast burritos or a smallish, corner restaurant on the Copperhill side. It was an easy decision on my part. I parked the car and headed inside the diner to take a peek at the menu.

From the look of it, the diner had been around for decades, and that was part of its charm. It had withstood flooding, financial hard times, and assorted tragedies that touched it all those years and closed down most of the other businesses. Large windows wrapped around the corner of the building and you could identify the older ones by the waviness of the blown-glass panes. Inside, the storefront diner was all high ceilings and slap-it-on whitewash. Some of the original features were still intact. The bar stools lined adjacent to the old Formica counter like black, leatherish mushrooms from a fairy tale book I'd read growing up. Black-and-white honeycomb tiles covered the floor, though the decades of parading shoes and boots and several floods had rendered a good number broken and sheenless, making them look tired.

The restaurant was narrow all the way to the back door, which you could see from the seating area. The bell on the door chirped as I entered, but no one was there to greet me so I slipped into a two-top table by a window so I could keep an eye on whatever was going on outside.

No one approached me, so I looked for a menu at the counter or on the other tables but found nothing. *Maybe they're closed*, I thought. I'd ventured in without noticing a sign on the door or window. At least ten minutes went by. I had just decided to stay a little while longer when I heard a small crashing in the back. Patiently, I waited to see what came next before calling it quits. I was hungry, and it was at least thirty minutes to another town.

A fortyish-year-old woman came out of the back like a bullet, leaving me in awe of the quickness of her entrance. She was all jeans, tenners, and a white T-shirt. She wasn't smiling, and I assumed that had to do with the crashing sound. She stopped when she saw me and just blinked my way for a minute, almost as though she were trying to blink me away. Like a little schoolgirl, I sat upright with my hands folded and an anxious fake smile on my face. I thought surely that was enough to make her play nice. Finally, she stopped blinking long enough to ask, "You need something?"

I spoke through my fake smile and tried to hold it together without becoming verbally combative. "Yes, you're open, right? I didn't see a sign on the door."

She rolled her shoulders and cracked her neck like a champion boxer in the ring before going in for the punch. "We're open."

All that effort and I got two words out of her. "Do you have a menu so I can order? I'm ready whenever you are, at your convenience."

She looked entertained and then all of the sudden, she wasn't. "Nope, we don't have one right now. What would you like? Hot tea and eggs with toast?"

Although it seemed like she was mocking me, I jumped on her offer and decided to take whatever she had in the back and hope she wasn't adding floor cleaner to it.

"That sounds wonderful. I'll take that and whatever else you suggest." With that she was gone, and I could hear clanking and scraping sounds from the kitchen. I continued to watch out the window, but there wasn't much going on that day.

My food arrived fairly quickly, and it looked safe, so I dug in and went up to the counter for refills of tea. After a half hour she asked if I was interested in iced tea, and I quickly said yes and asked for more toast. I sat there for another hour before I heard the phone on the wall ring. The server picked it up, and I heard chattering from the earpiece. It didn't take long before she came over to stand directly before me and asked what I was doing there.

My heart skipped a beat and I blinked hard at her. "I'm here looking around at the town. I'm interested in the Hicks Clinic. I was born there."

She sniffed at me and looked around as she spoke. "Are ya done with your plate? That'll be ten dollars. Cash."

I pulled the money out of my pocket and looked at her as I laid it down. And then I just sat there, stinging from the abruptness, trying to surmise what I had done or not done.

She took the cash and headed back toward the kitchen. Turning back to me just as she got to the kitchen doorway, she said something like, "I wouldn't suggest you ask about the clinic around here. The Hicks family has done a lot of good for folks."

Screeching my chair across the tile floor as I got up, I stood in wonder at the sensitivity to my presence, not sure if it was because I was an out-of-towner or because of my interest in the Hicks Clinic. I pulled a couple more dollars from my pocket and put them on the table, belting back at her, "I'll take that as friendly advice." Then I got out of there.

Aware that I stuck out like a sore thumb in these two towns and shaking my head at how quickly my innocence had exposed my Hicks Clinic secret to a stranger, I tried to shake it off and pick up the adventure. Out of the diner and on the main street again, I saw that it had turned into a beautiful day. I took my time walking down the street, soaking in the very, very small towns of Copperhill and McCaysville as I moved toward the clinic. Sidewalks lined both sides of the street, and storefronts for businesses, some long gone and some still holding on, caught my eye. I paid attention to the details. A building that must have been a barbershop or beauty salon from at least a decade ago now sat empty, its spinning chairs still anchored to the floor, forever stuck facing a long row of mirrors and countertops. The town head shop, which had wildly painted windows with a few diagonal cracks, looked frosted from the poor ventilation, and there was a smoky atmosphere inside. Across the street was a beer joint with a pool table and a bar. Some Harley-Davidsons were parked outside. Closer to the clinic and on the same side of the street was a stately dark brick house with a beautiful porch out front that didn't look like it was inhabited, maybe years ago but not that day.

Walking up to the Hicks Clinic was much more interesting and complicated than driving by. Weeds covered patches of the ground around the building and ran up against it in some places. I worked my way toward the foggy windows to take a peek inside, then pressed my forehead against the dirty glass. After my eyes adjusted to the closed-up rooms, I could see it was empty with a few piles of mildew-stained carpet and what looked like peeled wallpaper or drywall backing. Everything was covered in a layer of dirt and dust. The scent of decay was strong enough to smell from the outside. The building had been soaked in the last round of flooding and left to marinate in the southern heat.

I stood outside for a while, looking out at the town and trying to focus on what to do next. I was about to move somewhere else when I heard a voice close by and realized I was being watched.

In fact, I had been for a good amount of time. I had absolutely failed in countersurveillance.

"Do you have something on your mind, young lady? You've been standing out here for some time." The stranger was sweating profusely and, by the smell of it, had already taken some sips from the jug of moonshine in his hand. We were standing in broad daylight in the middle of the town for all to see, and he was asking me what I was pondering. That's how you could describe McCaysville back then, in short. It didn't matter what you asked of it, it was always going to question you for asking. I was learning that it was the John F. Kennedy of small towns. Ask not what the town could do for you, ask what you could do for the town.

I brushed my hair out of my eyes and put my hand up to fight off the glare of the oncoming morning sun. As hard as I tried, I couldn't take my eyes off the jug as he chatted away about Hicks and his clinic. The one thing I did catch was that the doctor had owned a farmhouse on the Georgia side, in addition to the clinic, and a house on the Tennessee side in Copperhill. The stranger told me to stay away from all of it before he meandered off with no explanation.

I spent the rest of the day driving between Copperhill, Mc-Caysville, and Blue Ridge, looking at the copper mine that stood on the edge of Copperhill very close to the railroad tracks. I also went to the library in Blue Ridge to look up newspaper articles. There were a few articles or, by the size of them, notations about Thomas Jugarthy Hicks, including obituaries for him and his son Walter. There was also a small article, only a couple paragraphs long, regarding a burglary at the Hicks residence in Copperhill in 1967. But I found nothing on an indictment or his losing his medical license. With no other appealing option, I called it a day and returned to the cemetery in Copperhill to watch the sunset before heading to my hotel room.

Hicks's crypt still reflected a little light as the sun was lowering in the sky, and in what was fast becoming my habit, I grabbed my quilt to get a front-row seat. Thinking of what had transpired that day, it hit me that I would have to prepare to battle for what was mine. Gathering information about the Hicks Clinic and my own origins would take more effort than I had anticipated, and for whatever reason, it was becoming clear my search for answers wouldn't be easy or welcome. The sunset covered my moves while I danced upon his grave that night. And I danced on his grave many times over the years, many sunsets ending like a Southern melody. To be clear, I wasn't stomping on his grave; I was dancing and telling him I was there.

"I'm here now, Doc. I know some of what you've done; now tell me what I need to know. Whatcha going to do now, Doc?" Those sunrises and sunsets were my contract with the search. They steeled me with hope of a new day and a chance encounter with truth to keep me moving forward. I needed to know who Doc Hicks was to find who I was, to find my birth story.

I was in no hurry to return to either the Fannin County Courthouse or the towns of McCaysville and Copperhill the next morning. So as I sat at the cemetery during the sunrise, I thought of the puzzle pieces that were missing, and Margaret Hicks swirled around in my head. At that time, most searches, obituaries, and gravesites gave the only concrete information to follow. Birth and death dates were for sure because family members could be confirmed by them. Obituaries gave enough information to get a good start on finding people, and I knew if I was going to find anyone from Doctor Hicks's obit, that left only his daughter.

The thought of tracking her down beat dealing with the ever-building crescendo of my unwelcome presence in town.

I found only one Margaret Hicks Brown who fit all the cor-relating information from my research. So I set my sights on an overnight trip to her home in North Carolina to knock on her door. I hoped for a better reception than I had received in Mc-Caysville. If anyone could help me, I was sure Margaret could. Well, I hoped so at least.

It was a beautiful North Carolina day with the sun shining and blue skies as though I had just driven onto a Hollywood movie set from the 1950s, all Audrey Hepburn and Cary Grant. The drive was uneventful, and I slowly made my way around the neighbor-hood, taking it in and looking for the address I had scrawled on the front of my notebook. When I found it, I smiled. The house was small but well presented with paint and landscaping. Some-one had an eye for detail. There was a screened-in porch jutting out from the side of the house that made me unsure if I was look-ing directly at the front door or not. The home didn't stick out in the quaint neighborhood as obnoxious or overdone; it was a perfect little house. It had green grass, some roses lining the path to the front steps, and a nice wooden door. The house number matched the address I had found in my research, and I started re-counting the conversations I had had with myself the entire drive from McCaysville. I felt ready for this encounter, come what may, and I began forming a mental checklist that seemed more suitable for hand-to-hand combat than a polite conversation.

Looking for a good place to settle near her house, I pulled over and parked on the street just in front. From the car, the stone walkway seemed a million miles away, and I closed my eyes to pray before getting out and walking up the steps. My mind focused on how quaint the house was, almost too cute for the intentions of the day. After one round of knocking, I waited for the door to open, hoping Margaret was home. Another round of knocking and finally a man answered the door. Smiling and trying to look angelic, I gleefully chirped, "Is Margaret home?"

With a tilt of the head, he disappeared, and a woman took his place a few moments later. She peeked out from around the door at me as my chirping started up again. I could see only her face since her body was hidden behind the door, but I started asking questions anyway. "Hi, my name is Jane, and I was hoping to talk to you about McCaysville. I was born at the Hicks Clinic, and I'm looking for information about my birth there."

With that, she stared at me with an almost glazed expression, thinking hard. We stood there just looking at each other. Me with a stupid, forced, nervous smile on my face and her surprised and contemplative. I'm not sure how long we were silent, but I remember it as an intense moment. Finally, she fully opened the door and let me in, gesturing to me to have a seat in the parlor that was separated from the rest of the house. She disappeared through a doorway for a few minutes as I sat there.

I looked around at the room steeped in tradition, high bookcases covering one wall with hundreds of dusty, leather-covered, and linen-lined books. The room was filled with antiques and older southern tchotchkes, like a trickling stream of pine and pineapple icons and Southern Belle images. My eyes adjusted to the surroundings and strained to see anything that could help, as though somehow clues might have been set before me, meticulously tucked into the bookcases or on the side table with the spindle legs. Fantasy pulled me into thinking Margaret would return with a ledger or box full of records, information I could use and find my name indexed within with a connection to my birth story. I dreamt that this connection to the Hicks Clinic would walk into the room with a box in her hands wrapped neatly and deliberately with a pretty satin bow on top just for me. That fantasy calmed me down and I waited, sitting quietly like the little girl decades before in her parents' living room, listening as they tried to explain what *black market* meant to a six-year-old. Anxious because of the unknown, as that same child I sat now, not knowing what to expect but hoping for a satin bow.

Margaret returned to the parlor and sat down in a comfortable chair across from me. I waited for her to speak. The initial moments were again tense and volatile as I waited for this stranger who held so much in her memory. I couldn't stay quiet for long with so many questions to ask.

Cautiously, I began. "As I said, I was born at the Hicks Clinic—both my sister and I, actually. I'm looking for help finding my birth family. I have nothing other than a birth certificate."

I watched her as she looked out the window, a musty, heavy haze lending to the intensity of my visit. This time the haze in the room wasn't cigarette smoke but the sunlight filtering through the large picture window. The dust of the front parlor added drama to the moment. She turned her eyes to me and spoke, simultaneously rapid-fire and formally. "You're the first one to come looking." She paused for a moment, as if to pull herself back from running at full speed, and then she began again, this time working to be a little more controlled.

She didn't ask how I found her. "I know what my father did. I know what was done." Tears welled in her eyes, and she took a few deep breaths. "I know and I'm sorry." And then she pulled the emotion back again.

My heart skipped a beat before settling down enough for me to think through what she had just said. From the stories they told in Copperhill, this was a woman with a hearty reputation for being a wild child. The accounts of her riding around the town in the nice car her daddy bought for her, drinking and painting the town her favorite color. The woman who was the town doctor's daughter with her always stylish clothes, always ready for an adventure with her beautifully coiffed hair and kittenlike smile, now sat before me, clad in matching polyester top and pants with crisp creases.

And she had said she was sorry. My mind was hurled into another world. I was confused and taken off guard by the apology for only God knows what. I barely whispered as if I was talking to myself. "You're sorry?"

She nodded and turned back to the window as she began to tell me what she knew about the babies. She never directly mentioned the abortions, but the tears flowed when she got close. She touched lightly on the women who came to her father for help, providing details to highlight that they needed assistance. Margaret kept calm and shared how her father worked hard for the town.

She was still halfway neutral and coy about the details of her father's business as the tears streamed down her face. She was a daddy's girl, and the words seemed hard to say as she talked about the farmhouse on the Georgia side, not far from McCaysville, and the Tennessee house on the hill that overlooked the two towns. She mentioned the Hicks Clinic and its nursery with the babies lined up in bassinets. I sat amazed and caught up in the careful and deliberate method of her storytelling and lost track of my agenda.

After a short time of reminiscing about McCaysville and Copperhill and the years of her growing up there, she finally turned to look me square in the face to make sure I heard her words. With tears still moist on her cheeks, she spoke in a tone less formal and more intimate, giving me the disclaimer again. "I've come to know God now, and I know what my daddy did was wrong. And I'm not the same person I used to be." I didn't know what to say, so after a few moments, I asked if I could contact her later with more questions.

She quietly said yes as tears covered her face again in a steady stream. She was still looking straight at me, never taking her eyes off me as I stood and whispered my thanks and headed toward the door.

On the way out I didn't notice the walkway or the flowers on the path and I don't remember how I figured out how to get from the street to the highway. I just drove, not caring where I was going and overwhelmed by where I'd just been. I turned the music on, blasting Springsteen, and just drove. It wasn't until a few hours later that I made the decision to head back to Ohio instead of returning to McCaysville. I needed to retreat for a while to emotionally recharge. I needed to look at the information gathered on this trip and begin to strategically push those puzzle pieces toward one another to see what fit and what didn't.

SIX

And Other Stories

I SMILE WHEN I THINK BACK ON how naive I was when I first started my investigation. No one warned me, and I'm pretty sure it wouldn't have mattered. Stupidity and blind foolishness had nothing on me when I was following a lead. With two years of searching in McCaysville under my belt, the things I'd learned about Hicks were definitely not a bread crumb trail, but the tracks were getting clearer with every North Georgia adventure.

After yet another day of traveling from the north to the south to start the search again and a good night's rest at the hotel, I spent the morning at the cemetery, sitting next to the Hicks mausoleum, watching the sunrise, waiting for the day to start before making my way back to the diner in Copperhill. The sting of my first visit two years ago was gone, erased by my desire to find more and push back. I had the gloves on again.

He leaned across the counter, rested on one arm, and looked me up and down twice before asking if I wanted a menu. When I said yes, he handed me a piece of paper, and I looked at it with suspicion. The last time I was in here, they didn't have a menu, so this was a step up. The interior had the same high ceilings, but there were a few newer dishes. The inside was cleaner, and sounds were coming out of the kitchen at a more robust level. The barstools were still lined up in front of the counter, and the black-and-white honeycomb floor remained, but the tiles didn't look as tired.

The menu had the daily offerings penciled in, and I quickly decided on my meal. While we waited for my food, the server asked me what I was doing in Copperhill, and I told him I was just looking around at McCaysville mostly. I couldn't tell him I was sightseeing because the town was so pretty. It wasn't, and he'd know for sure I was lying. He mumbled a bit at me as he placed a porcelain café plate on the table in front of me. "Not sure why you needed to come all the way here from Oh-hi-o. Nothing to find here, really."

My eyes focused on the eggs and toast while he returned to the counter and wiped the top again, talking to me the whole time. While he chattered away, I focused on a strategy, thinking of my next move through McCaysville and Copperhill and to the Hicks Clinic.

I cut through his discussion of clean floors and the best paper towels with a question. "What do you know about the Hicks Clinic?"

He paused, seeming taken aback, a moment before responding. "I know it's been closed down for some time. Decades, actually. Why?"

I met his eyes. "Just wondering. I'm doing research about the area and it keeps coming up. Plus, the building is just sitting there empty, and I was wondering about it."

A smile crossed his face like he was proud of his thoughts. He artistically and unapologetically uttered the next word as though he were on a stage in NYC, playing to the audience of a Broadway show. "Bulova."

"Bulova?" I repeated. "Like the watch?" My brows furled as I tried to figure out what he was getting at.

He chirped back to me. "Yes, the watch."

That was a put-your-fork-down moment if I'd ever run across one. What followed was either going to be very good or a waste of my time. So I put my fork down and looked at him as he kept going. These are the stories he told, as I recall them.

"Doc Hicks ran the place and was known for a few things—mostly that he was a funny, odd man who had a lot of money and such, considering he was the town doctor. He had many opportunities to take from patients he tended to before the families claimed them or got them moved to the funeral parlor. And he took those opportunities. One man he tended to had a brand-new Bulova watch on, and they say it was a real nice one too. Everyone knew he had it on when he died. Next thing you know, the doctor had a real nice Bulova watch and was showing it off all over town."

I was chuckling at the thought of such a scoundrel and barely got out a reply because of the comedy of it all. My face screwed up as I managed to ask, "You saw it?"

"Naw, my daddy saw it though. I was too young back then to know. He was a real character, he was. Hicks was a character, not my daddy. There's a story about another man he did the same way." The phone on the wall began to ring obnoxiously, and he turned to get it.

"Diner, whatcha need?" He belted into the receiver. "Mm-hmm. Yes. Mm-hmm. No, we got that last week." Then he hung up the phone, banging it on the wall like he meant it.

I was thoughtfully eating and not sure if the conversation was safe to start again, so I stayed quiet to see what was next. I didn't have to wait long. He moved toward my table to continue the recollections.

"There was another story, and it was a real funny one. Not sure when it happened but everyone in town and even some folks in Chattanooga knew about it. Hicks was known for some doozies, for sure."

I listened to him as he shook with laughter at the stories he'd heard from others in his family and around town over the years. The way he told the stories brought them to life so much that I could picture them in my own mind.

It was cleanup time for Doc Hicks after a challenging day. The night before was a long, drawn-out mess of pneumonia the patient didn't recover from, and the doctor was tired. Scrubbing his hands and then up midway to his elbows for assurances' sake had become a good habit of his to ensure he didn't catch anything. First thing they teach you when you want to be a doctor. There were too many patients to take care of to miss days being sick. His assistant couldn't handle everything; she was a good nurse but was not always on top of everything, in his opinion. He was the one in charge and had to make sure it stayed that way.

He looked over at the dead man's body and thought about how quickly he deteriorated, how unexpected it was for a fairly young, healthy man to die of pneumonia. He looked at the suit the man had on when he came into his office; it was draped across a chair. His family was in town and would return to the clinic soon to pay for Hicks's services. He heard someone in the front of the building and guessed it was the funeral home he had called to pick up the deceased.

"Is that you? Come on back," Hicks called. "He's here in the back room." The funeral home worker made his way to Hicks and made quick work of gathering the man and his effects. Everything was gone within a half hour. The worker asked Doc Hicks to come up to the funeral home after the service and sign some paperwork and be a witness before he shut the casket the final time. Doc Hicks agreed and went home to get some sleep. His staff would take the helm for a few hours.

A couple days later, Doc Hicks made his way to the funeral home to inspect the unfortunate man. He stood alone in the room looking at the man in the casket in his nice suit, a faint smile placed on his face by the mortician. The service was over, the family had paid their respects, and the burial was the only thing left. Hicks looked the dead man over and noticed he was a bit bulky. His waist was stouter than it had been. Before Hicks signed the paperwork, he asked about the bulk. They told him the man had designated a few specifics about his burial in his will. He wanted to be buried with all the wealth he had, amounting to a sizable number of cash bundles that were placed around his midsection. Doc Hicks signed the paperwork attesting to the man's demise but stayed for a moment, lingering without supervision. Unbuttoning the suit jacket for just a peek, Hicks saw the stack of bills, and he couldn't let such an opportunity pass. He decided what was in his best interests, and within moments, left to make his way back to the Hicks Clinic.

One last mandatory check on the deceased brought the funeral worker back into the room before sealing the casket.

Opening the lid, he noticed the suit jacket was unbuttoned and the body appeared less bulky. Upon further inspection, his eyes landed on a small, cream-colored slip laying across the man's now-concave belly. His jaw dropped as he picked it up and looked closer. All of the bundles of cash had been replaced by a check made out to the deceased by Thomas Jugarthy Hicks.

The funeral home worker hurried to his office to call Hicks, sweat breaking out across his forehead and the bridge of his nose at the thought of what this would do to his reputation and his business. He ringed the phone operator and, once connected, started the conversation hard and quick. "My word, Thomas, bring the money back. I have to bury him within the next half hour. The family's waiting right now. That's what he wanted, and you have no right to steal from a dead man. My word, what was I thinking leaving you with a dead body? Do we have to watch every last move with you?"

Hicks responded, "Now, he ain't gonna use it, that's for sure. Go on and do your business. No one knows but you, and you shouldn't hear nothin' about it."

When he finished the funeral home story, we both laughed at the crazy-like-a-fox role Doc Hicks took, if that was the truth of what happened. I had cleaned my plate, poured myself another cup of hot tea from the carafe, and brushed the crumbs off my lap by the time he ran out of stories.

While listening, I thought of a few good questions. "Do you know anything about adoptions out of the Hicks Clinic?"

He just looked at me and cocked his head. "You mean abortions, right?" I shook my head. No one had directly mentioned the abortions before, though there had been hints.

"No," I said, "adoptions."

He rubbed his chin. "Ain't never heard of adoptions from there. Abortions and Hicks having himself a good time with all the ladies is what it's known for. Never heard of anything else, really. Except some people said he kept babies in jars, but I don't believe that much. Who would do that? And what for?" He paused for a moment and thought about it. "What makes you think there were adoptions?"

Still not sure what to tell him and what to keep close as I thought of the first breakfast in the diner, I shrugged and mumbled that I'd heard it somewhere. He left to grab my check and came back a few minutes later.

He was grinning and started talking about the times Margaret Hicks ran roughshod over the towns when she was in her teens, feeling out what life had to offer her. "She was a hot potato to handle, from what they say. But she was the doc's little girl, and he raised her to know her place, a mighty high place around here." He stopped again as he did throughout our conversation and thought for a bit before giving some more details of Margaret and who she was still connected to in town. He laid out her story and lineage in such detail, it rivaled the genealogies in the Bible.

His stories reminded me that Margaret had mentioned the Hicks farmhouse, so, since I had time, I asked him for directions. He told me the house was up past the curve on Highway 60, about two miles ahead and to the right. No landmarks. It wasn't apparent to him that I was not used to those kinds of instructions. I simultaneously heard his directions and pictured myself getting lost. I threw my hands up, figured I'd wing it, and thanked him before heading back to my car to take a drive to find the farmhouse.

Winding my way on the route as directed, juggling driving and reading road signs, I was hopeful. Blind hope and not knowing what I was getting into fueled my steps most of the time. Only God kept me from trouble, and sometimes I tempted Him with my inexperience. I'd found the street sign and followed it up a narrow dirt road surrounded by high grass, wildflowers, and some spots of out-of-control weeds. Driving farther off the main road, I questioned if I was on the right road and if I was doing a smart thing versus a dumb thing. The road narrowed even more, and some gravel had been spread out at the end of a driveway just a few feet farther. There were a couple houses some distance away from each other, nothing you could throw a stone at and hit, and at least a dog or two barking at the sound of my tires, because they were too lazy to come see what I was doing.

Two farmhouses were ahead. One with a small barn and the other with a decent-sized front porch. The second was obviously vacant. The outside needed paint, and weeds threatened to overtake it. Windows were cracked and some fenceposts were missing from the perimeter. But it was sitting in a beautiful spot, and wildflowers grew around the house and over the hills behind it. Every so often a patch of wild roses hinted at life at the farmhouse not too, too long ago. The other house was smaller and possibly inhabited, although I didn't see anyone around. I got out of my car and took off toward the seemingly abandoned house to poke around and see if I could trespass a bit but not enough to get into any trouble.

Looking into the front windows and walking around back, even with a flashlight I couldn't get a good look at anything, and although the hinges on the doors ran ragged and pulled from the wooden jambs, they were shut up good enough, keeping me from a Title 16 misdemeanor as outlined in Georgia state law for criminal trespass. Keeping an eye out for any breach drew me to the foundation and further visual assessment. Excitement welled up inside me when I saw that one of the basement windows was smashed. I wiggled my way to the ground to look inside but was deflated when I saw nothing of any interest. My mind soared with hope that records would be stored somewhere, and this would be a likely place. If it were only so simple. My obsession with finding a box of records was beginning to feel more like an addiction. Hopes dashed, I pulled myself up with adrenaline pumping through me from the mystery of it all. For no real reason, I skipped back to my car, holding on to the black tactical bag I brought with me to hold my flashlight and other MacGyver-like tools not worth mentioning. Halfway to the car, I heard someone moving behind me, not right behind me, but it stopped me in my tracks. Adrenaline still pumping, I slowly looked around but didn't see anyone. The dogs were still lounging and didn't seem to care about me. I started to slowly move to the car again, hoping to get out of there, when I heard someone ask me what I needed.

Looking around and still not seeing anyone, I raised my voice and answered that I was looking for the Hicks farmhouse. Still not out in the open so I could see them, with a growling voice, they responded, "You found it, now go."

In the blur of everything and with my heart in high gear, I thought I heard a shotgun racking, a sound that has its own universal language to those skipping across a stranger's front yard, no matter which state you happen to be in. I don't make a habit of questioning that sound. I go on faith that I should leave it be. So I moved to my car as quickly as I could, caught a quick breath, and hit the gas, spinning the tires as I pulled onto the dirt road and flew like a banshee from the farmhouse back to town.

Walking back into the diner and shaking a bit, I slid into a chair and threw my head back to stare at the ceiling for a minute to get my bearings. I soon found out the gentleman who was so helpful before had ended his shift. The new server was nice enough, but I didn't want to take any more chances. After a little chitchat, I left the diner and headed back to the not-so-mean streets of Copperhill and McCaysville, looking for a quiet place to sit and think.

Rummaging through my notes while walking was a challenge for me. It may have been the storm clouds rolling in or a delayed reaction to the farmhouse event, but I stumbled over a clump of weeds growing between the cracks of the concrete, spilling everything in my hands and flinging my purse to the ground. The spectacle caught the attention of a cop sitting in his police car across the street, and he eyed me, half suspicious and half amused. Brushing myself off and working hard to stand upright, I nodded to the cop and continued walking, moving closer and with hope of making it past him with some dignity. My face was warm with embarrassment, but I was not daunted, so I all but stuck my tongue out in defiance and kept heading toward the real goal of the day.

Margaret had told me about growing up in the big house on the corner across from the Copperhill town hall, which was tucked in among the other houses built on the steep hills overlooking the town. Thomas Hicks's house was up to the left off the main street and across the railroad tracks. It stood out not because of its size or features but because it jutted out of the landscape like the hull of a ship on the horizon, leading and purposeful. I ran my eyes over every detail as I drew closer to the house, noting every window and door, the eaves above the porch, and the semi-run-down condition of its structure. Somehow the past had released the house of its responsibilities of presentability, and it seemed to have let go just in the past decade. I would have mistaken it for empty if not for the sign on the front porch indicating a restaurant was inside. It was open and, in a split second, my feet made their way up the concrete steps and into the house. The house that had belonged to the Hicks family.

It was dark at first when I entered, and I fumbled a bit as I surveyed my surroundings. The rough wood floors needed a good sanding and finish; the years had taken their toll. There was a sweet aroma in the air, filling the place with comfort. A nice lady showed me to a cloth-clad table with a petite glass bud vase filled with a lone daisy. She explained that I had arrived at a good time and told me the special of the day, marinated chicken and noodles with a side of biscuits. My table was right next to the mantel, and I was the only customer.

I was still taking it all in when she handed me silverware, gave directions to the bathroom, then promptly left for the kitchen. I had wanted quiet and now I had it, but I was too caught up in the place, too fully engaged to relax. I did a 360 of the rooms within my sight. Nice windows and a stairway off to the side. The floral wallpaper on some of the walls and wood trim everywhere were tributes to the solid build of the house and the beauty of the era in which it was built.

When the woman returned with a glass of water and caught me looking around, she asked where I was from, and we chatted for a bit. I selected the special and a glass of sweet tea. I learned that the server was also the owner. She was renting the space for the restaurant, but she wanted to make it into a bed-and-breakfast. She told me I could look around while she got the food ready if I wanted, and I jumped at the opportunity.

To be in Hicks's house was monumental. And the food was a bonus. With this turn of events, I was forced to get my mental bearings for the fifth time that day. I started fumbling my way through, room by room, and hummed to mask my nervousness as I turned a corner straight into a doorway. I was dumbfounded and stood looking at it without moving, not sure if I was even breathing.

The old wooden door had a frosted glass window that had DOCTOR splayed across it in faded and peeling black lettering, which was almost completely gone. My heart was beating hard and what seemed too loud as I reached out to open it. But it was shut up tight. I tried twisting and jostling the doorknob to get it to open to no avail. Immersed in the door, I didn't notice that my server passed by with a steaming-hot plate of food and then backtracked to scrutinize what I was doing, lingering until I turned to humbly follow her back to the table.

Over the next thirty minutes, her gaze was fixed on me, and I worked hard with every thread of my being to smile every time her eyes met mine or she asked me if I needed anything. That door was too much to look away from now for either of us. Midway through my marinated chicken and on the hundredth time she checked on me and filled my glass of sweet tea, I told her I was from the Hicks Clinic. With that she sighed and sat down and listened as I outlined my adoption story and my desire to find my birth family. She chuckled when I mentioned Hicks and said he was known for many things, but she was too young to know what he was really doing all those years ago. The door was locked because the property owner had personal effects in there. But she suggested I go upstairs and look around at the bedrooms.

The upstairs quelled none of my curiosity in comparison to the door with the lettering and the mystery of what was in that room. I soon found myself back at the table, lingering as long as I could without getting kicked out, though I was still the only customer. It had been an eventful day that had left me emotionally exhausted and physically aching for a nice soft spot to fall into. I left the wonder of Doc Hicks's house behind, but the details of the once-polished rooms, the smell of extraordinary Southern food, the rough wooden floor that needed a shine, and the frosted glass window were now neatly captured in my mind like old photos, snapshots of Hicks's life.

SEVEN

Walls Crumbled

AFTER TAKING IN ANOTHER SUNRISE at the cemetery, I spent most of the next day driving around, getting a feel for some of the outlying towns on the Tennessee side. Isabella, Ducktown, Turtletown, and up far around Coker Creek and then winding around to the Nantahala National Forest until I hit Sweetwater and turned around. It had been another long day, and I was looking for something more. I had stories of Hicks, lore of the town, and some downright good gossip but nothing to help me find my birth mother. I needed more. I always needed more. And on this day in McCaysville, undoubtedly one of the smallest towns I knew of, I was back to struggling with directions. Long before GPS was installed in every car and long before mobile phones were around to redirect, I was fumbling with a folded paper map of Georgia. There were no local versions that I could get my hands on, and I needed help with the roads before heading back to my hotel in Blue Ridge. A couple more stops and I'd be through for the day. A couple more stops and, hopefully, another lead to follow.

I drove around the town looking for a good place to ask for directions. Even though it was the early afternoon, most of the few stores were closed for the day, and the guy at the gas station had seen plenty of me over the last few days, so that was not a good choice. Finally, I spotted a small building just off the main road, a building that housed several businesses by the looks of it. As I rounded the corner and looked for a parking spot, I noticed a tiny florist shop. Not sure if it was open or not, I parked in the space in front of the door and headed in. Worst-case scenario I would buy some flowers to tote around with me and gain some solid driving directions to the destinations on the next day's to-do list.

The door of the shop was heavy, but it swung wide open and a bell chattered from above as I crossed the threshold. The smell of flowers was overwhelming and stopped me for a minute as I absorbed the goodness of that spot where I was standing. It felt dewy in the shop, and everything was saturated in sweetness. It was as though I was standing in a garden after a light rain, before the sun dried every drop away. Gardens are my loves, and I felt revived as the bell on the door chattered away as it swung back and forth from my entrance.

No one was out front when I arrived. There was a counter and rows of flowers in a chilled-air cabinet and plants hanging from the walls. There was also what looked like a backroom directly behind the left side of the counter. I squeaked out a hello like any self-respecting B-horror movie actress about to regret her weekend of camping and moved closer to the counter. Like a flash, a man came out of the backroom. He didn't look happy, and he belted out a question I wasn't prepared for. "How'd you get in here?"

"Through the door."

"No, you didn't."

Not sure what was happening, I answered, "Um, yes, I did."

He wasn't convinced. "You couldn't have. How'd you get in here?"

I reiterated as nicely as I could. "I told you. Through this door."

He looked at me and wasn't any happier than when he first set eyes on me. "No, we locked that door an hour ago, and it was shut up good." He stood there.

A woman joined him from a backroom and nicely confirmed the door had been locked. I stood there for a few minutes that felt closer to at least an hour and was more worried about it being locked now and me not getting away from these two than I was about it being locked before I came in. That was a detail I had nothing to do with and yet there I was in their shop. The only upside to the uneasiness was I could still smell the sweetness of the flowers all around me.

The two florists were looking at me, sizing me up.

The man started. "How can we help you? You're not from here, are you?"

All of the sudden I was worried what they would think of my objective. Other than flowers, what would I tell them I was looking for?

"No, I'm in town and writing a book about McCaysville, thought I'd check to see if you—"

He cut me off quickly. "No, you're not. Why don't you tell me what you're really doing here? What you want? You're not a writer." He looked right through me and didn't look away.

I closed my eyes for a few seconds and then took a breath and told him everything. The woman who had come out of the backroom earlier gave him a long, worried look before retreating behind the counter and backing out of sight.

"Uh-huh. I see. The Hicks Clinic?" He seemed to hesitate before asking, "What year?"

"I was born in January 1965, and my sister, Michelle, was born in 1961."

"You been talking to other townsfolk?"

"Only a few. And I told them I was a researcher/writer. Didn't tell all of them that I was born at the clinic. They didn't say much."

He looked out the side window then back at me. "I may be able to help you a little, but you can't go around telling people. I have a business to keep and some people don't like questions about Doc Hicks or the Hicks Clinic. Do you understand?"

"Yes, I do." I stood waiting for my mission with no question, I was willing to take it.

He tore off a piece of paper from a notepad and wrote down an address and phone number and handed it to me. "I'm Frank, and that's my wife. Wait 'til later, closer to dark, and come up to the house. We can talk there." His face was full of genuine concern, and a small bit of worry.

With that, I thanked him, and he warned me not to get too happy since he wasn't sure what he could help with quite yet. But I was just happy to have found someone who would listen. I went out the door that had been locked with no problems and didn't wait to see if it would be sealed up after I left. The bell was chattering again, and with my windows rolled down, I could hear it as I backed out of the parking spot. Smiling and thinking of the sweet sound of the bell as the flowers swirled around in my head. Now I just had to wait for later, for the evening.

⸻

The drive to their house was simple enough, and I made my way using Frank's directions, taking a few breaths behind the wheel of the car. I was not sure of what I was going to hear, if anything, but something felt different about this, different from the others I had talked to at the diner. Finally, I swung my feet out of the car and headed to the front door. We said our hellos, and I kept thinking how nice they were as Frank's wife directed me to the living room where he was reading the newspaper and waiting.

He spoke quietly and I sat on the couch and listened as he asked questions and I filled him in on what I knew already. I told him about the diner incidents and walking up on the porch next to the Hicks's farmhouse, almost falling into the farmhouse basement window. I'd have thought he surely felt sorry for me if he hadn't been grinning the whole time I told him of my shenanigans. His wife listened intently, filling our glasses with some of the best sweet tea I've ever had. Frank was gauging me to see not only what I knew but also what I could handle.

Overall, it was a breakthrough evening, and I was thankful I had walked into the florist shop that afternoon. It was the first of several conversations with Frank about the Hicks Clinic and McCaysville, and his guidance was key to most of everything I've done with my searching. But the stories Frank told me of what Doctor Hicks did were the most sobering I've heard in my lifetime.

Frank had lived most of his life in McCaysville and had worked in many capacities: furniture and appliance delivery person, ambulance driver, jack-of-all-trades, and, when needed, hired help at the funeral home. He was a credible source and he was straight with me, and that meant the world. I would ask him a question or two and he would tell me yes or no and sometimes he would give me the story as he personally saw it, or he'd share a firsthand account from family, friends, or coworkers. I left his house on overload that first night, so very grateful for the God of unlocking florist shop doors.

On my next trip to Georgia, several months later, I was back at Frank's house for another question-and-answer session, and he was relaying some stories for me based on my inquiries. My jaw was resting almost completely on my chest as though it had dropped like an anvil when he told me about Prissy and Irwin, two young siblings who bore the bond, and sometimes pain, of being family to each other as they made their way through this world.

Frank's words were clear and hit dead center, but I had a hard time absorbing them.

I wanted to know why and how Hicks had quit practicing on the Georgia side and what the court had to do with it. I knew he had done prison time and lost his license in Tennessee for selling drugs, but not enough on the Georgia legal issues Hicks faced. "Do you know why they indicted him? I understand that abortions were illegal at that time, but what do you know about the details? Were there any indications that it could've been something else?"

Frank got halfway through the story and then saw the look on my face. I must have seemed confused because he stopped for a few minutes while I caught up to the meaning of what he'd said. When I did, it was my turn to sit quietly and wait for him to finish framing the story. He had been hesitant about sharing in the beginning but must have realized I needed his help and his memories of Doc Hicks and the town. He wasn't just a source; he was the best source. A good man and a stabilizing factor in my search. Here is the story of Prissy and Irwin as I envisioned it from his account.

PRISSY AND IRWIN

The view from the car window was limited. Smudges from the top of Prissy's head as it bobbed with the motion of the car marked the glass, creating a blur and isolating her even further from the rest of the outside world. It was dark outside, too early for the sun to be up. The trees and roadside gas stations whizzed by at a speed she didn't want to guess, making her stomach churn. She looked over at her brother, hearing his words every so often but blocking out the majority of the lecture.

"I told you this would happen. Momma would be ashamed if she knew what you've been up to."

His ranting continued as she retreated into her own world. But soon she had had enough, and she stopped his words short. "Momma's dead." Silence.

Finally, silence. He couldn't dispute her words. Their momma was gone, and nothing would change that fact or bring her back to them.

Pulling up to a brick building on Highway 5 in McCaysville, they looked hard through the dark at the sign in the front window. HICKS CLINIC. That was it. The doctor had said it was brick and square, and the sign settled it. There was nothing left to do except go in and tell them they had arrived. A friend of Irwin's knew a man who said Doc Hicks could help them determine what needed to be done.

Priscilla had never been to a doctor before. At least, not a woman's doctor. She was not yet eighteen years old and she was pretty. Irwin was her double with the same hair and eyes. Their parents had passed, and now Irwin and Prissy carried on the family alone.

She put one foot out of the car, slow and deliberate. She knew the moment would come when a doctor would have to look at her and decide how far along she was, even though she knew precisely when it had happened. It was at a church social with her boyfriend. They had snuck away from the rest of the congregation for a walk and ended up in the back of his uncle's '55 something or another. He was her sweetheart, but she never thought about being touched by him. Or at least, not like that, not until she felt him on top of her and felt his breathing.

She spoke under her breath as she struggled to stand up. "God, if only I'd have talked to Momma when she asked. If only I understood the bees."

"What'd you say, Prissy?" Irwin's voice caught her by surprise as he came to help her out of the car.

"The bees, Irwin. Just thinkin' about bees, is all."

He caught her arm, helped her up, and shook his head. He'd never understand women.

The two siblings looked at each other and knew this was not what should be done. They could get through this together. But there would be gossip and maybe even some words with the pastor. A light went on in the building, and they both turned to look.

Irwin tried to fight the urgency in his voice. "Prissy, you don't have to do this. I'm sorry I brought you here. We can figure out something else." Irwin was old enough to be Prissy's guardian and the baby's too.

Doc Hicks came to the door to greet his visitors, motioning them to come in. Prissy just looked at him and smiled faintly.

"Come on, Irwin. We'll talk to him."

They entered the building and followed Hicks down the hall and into his office. He sat down in his leather chair and directed them to join him. "We've been expecting you. How was the trip? It wasn't too bad, was it?"

Irwin wasn't the most confident man and diverted his eyes away from Doc Hicks. Everything was coming apart, and he was supposed to be the one in charge. "No, sir, it wasn't."

Hicks asked over his morning coffee, "So what can I do for you?"

Prissy sat up straight in her chair. She looked at Irwin. He was older, but Prissy was the stronger of the two. He looked a mess with his eyes glued to the floor as fear enveloped him.

She moved her body hard against the cold metal chair, gripping it for strength before speaking. "I thought I wanted to have you help me about a pregnancy, but now I'm not sure. I think I'm about four months along, so I think I want to just have an exam."

"You don't look four months along." A pause. "How are you going to keep the baby?" Hicks looked sideways at Irwin. "Do you have a job, young man?"

Irwin snapped to attention and gave a stiff-lipped reply. "I have a job at the farm and Momma left us the house." He sank back into his chair in nervous, quiet surrender.

Hicks seemed confused. "Momma? Are you two married?"

Prissy was irritated with Irwin and answered in his place. "No, sir. Irwin and I are sister and brother. He's not the father."

Hicks moved uncomfortably forward in his chair as if he was in pain. "Oh. You're putting yourself in a bit of a position, aren't ya? Folks don't look kindly on young girls running around without husbands."

Prissy looked him in the eyes and clarified her newly solidified intent. "I don't want an abortion."

The doctor appeared to contemplate the situation as he looked them over. Perhaps it seemed to him right then that she was older than she'd said. Sitting back in his chair and locking his hands behind his head, he rocked back and forth, looking from one to the other in assessment, making them even more nervous and on edge.

He carefully presented the next round of the conversation. "I don't think you should keep this baby. Have it and I'll find a nice home for it."

Prissy hadn't thought about putting the baby up for adoption, and it hit her. Her stomach lurched, and she threw her hands to her mouth. Irwin reached out, placing a hand on her back to comfort her.

Hicks didn't miss a beat and went on to explain further. "I'd offer for you to stay here at the clinic to work off the fee, but I haven't been feeling well lately, and we're not as busy as once before. But you can come back to have the baby. The time will fly by, and then you can get back to your life as it was before. Girls do that here all the time."

Prissy was on the verge of panicking and stated the obvious to Hicks again. "You don't understand. I want this baby. I've changed my mind." She looked at Irwin, and he nodded in agreement. It was the right thing to do.

Hicks sucked on his lower lip and kept rocking, looking between them once more. "Well, then, let's look at ya. We'll see how far along you are, at least. Young man, you can wait in the lobby while we get a room ready."

Prissy looked to Irwin, questioning the fear and the desire to run away from it all that was rising in her. The doctor motioned for them to leave, and they headed to the front of the building and had a seat in the lobby to wait.

―――――――――

The lobby was quiet. Metal chairs lined up in a row against the front window made it feel like a card party. Prissy turned her chair to face the glass as they sat waiting. She could see her reflection in the window as the morning sun mirrored her. She looked tired and scared. Tears wouldn't come even now. She had made a decision to keep the baby and not turn her back on what she believed, like her momma had taught her. It'd be okay, maybe tough, but it would be okay.

Irwin was feeling better too. They would be all right. An older lady came over to them. "The doctor will see you now, miss. Come with me."

Prissy turned to Irwin and smiled before following the nurse down the hall into the examining room. "You can undress from the waist down. Remove your underthings too. Then you can get on the table. The doctor will be here in a minute," the lady instructed Prissy before she left the room.

Prissy undressed quickly, counting the days since the church social. It had been about four months; she was nearly halfway through. She lay on the table against the hard metal and stared at the tile on the walls. The room smelled of ammonia and lemons. About twenty minutes passed before the doctor appeared with his assistant trailing close behind, closing the door as she entered.

"I know how far along I am. About four months." Prissy nervously blurted the only real detail she felt comfortable discussing.

Hicks responded, "You don't look four months along. You're too thin, and your belly is too small." He sized her up. "We'll see. Slide down on the table." He motioned for his assistant to help Prissy position herself at the end of the examination table and keep her covered by the sheet. As soon as Prissy was settled in the right place, the nurse left to tend to something else.

Hicks lifted the draped sheet, proceeding to further assess her pregnant belly. She was right. The doctor shook his head, cussing under his breath and mumbling as he put direct pressure on her cervix.

Prissy screamed from the pain and pushed her legs against the bottom platform of the table her feet had been resting on, pushing away from Hicks. He pulled back fast and scowled at her as she lay there, shaking and dazed in pain.

Hicks yelled at her. "You should lay still! Let me do my work!"

Prissy let out a cry, going limp on the table as Hicks moved to the door, wiping his hands, now slightly bloody. He opened the door a crack and hollered for his nurse to join him.

She entered just seconds later to hear him say, "This is going to be harder than I thought; the baby is further along." He turned back to Prissy and nonchalantly said, "You shouldn't keep this baby, and you know it."

Prissy was horrified, immobilized by fear and confusion. She could only lay there crying quietly as Hicks gave more directions to his assistant.

"Hold on to her arms and keep her still. Be quiet, young lady, do you hear me?"

Prissy moaned in pain as the doctor pressed deeper, opening her womb. The urge to push took over as she relied on panting to get through. When Hicks was finishing up and it was almost over, she laid still, numb and cold as he talked to the nurse.

"She'll thank me for this later," he said. Then he was gone, leaving the nurse to clean up.

The sound of stainless steel pans clattering together brought Prissy back to full consciousness. She looked over the side of the table to the blood- and urine-stained sheets piled on the floor, the smell rising to her nostrils.

"Take this and you'll feel better. Here's some water to get it down," the nurse said, handing Prissy a pill and a glass of water.

Prissy struggled to sit up without falling off the table, her head was spinning. She took the pill and swallowed as hard as she could, her throat almost swollen shut from the strain of the ordeal she'd just experienced.

Through a haze, Prissy heard the nurse's last instructions. "You can get dressed now. When you're ready, you can leave. If the bleeding doesn't stop in a few days, go to a hospital."

———————————

Hicks came out to the lobby and called Irwin to his office. The young man returned to the back of the building and sat down in front of the doctor's desk. His services would cost one hundred dollars. Irwin wouldn't understand the full meaning of the bill until he saw Prissy later. He paid the fee and Hicks stood, signaling him to return to the waiting area. As Irwin approached the door, he heard the doctor's voice from behind. "If there is anything else I can do for ya, let me know."

———————————

Irwin was sitting anxiously in the lobby an hour later when Prissy came out. He didn't know what had taken her so long after Hicks was done with her. She was hunched over and shuffling slowly across the floor. He saw her wrecked body, the bruises on her arms, and then he knew something horrible had happened. He rushed to his sister, and she collapsed in his arms, so he picked her up and carried her to the car. They sat in silence for a few minutes as Irwin caught up with reality. Prissy sat with her head hanging, her chin almost resting on her chest.

Softly, Irwin spoke. "What did he do?"

She could barely think of what had just happened. It hurt to speak. "The baby is dead, Irwin. He took my baby."

He let out a gasp and looked at Prissy. Her face was swollen, and tiny veins had burst across her cheeks. Their gazes locked on each other until Irwin couldn't look at her anymore. He grasped the steering wheel, laid his head against it, and sobbed. Prissy slumped against the door and grieved with him. Five months later, on what could have been her baby's birthday, Priscilla walked into the sheriff's office and asked to speak to someone.

I heard Frank finish the story through a fog. Then he asked, "Are you ready for more?" Silence from me. I just sat there. He repeated the question, and I was finally able to tear my mind away from what I'd just heard. I managed to stutter. "He forced an abortion?"

Frank nodded. "That's what I was told. And I can tell you more, just let me know."

I took a moment to process the nature of what he'd just re-layed, and then nodded for him to keep going. He matter-of-factly filled in details of the complainant as he had been told the story from one of the jurors on the panel. And I sat in disbelief, listening, and at some points, almost wishing my best source of information was mistaken. But I knew he wasn't. He knew McCaysville, the roads, the businesses, the people, the goings-on. He had started the story to answer my question, so I sat there and took it in, not as an investigator but as another baby sold from the hands of the same doctor who played God at his whim. Prissy's struggle was heart-wrenching and horrific, and she did nothing to deserve how she was treated. She was just run over by a force she couldn't fight and made to feel worthless and voiceless. It was too much of a struggle to pretend I had no stake in this story. That baby could have been me.

EIGHT

Friend of the Family

WE FINISHED OUR CONVERSATION about Prissy and Irwin that night. The next day, Frank called and referred me to an older lady in town who had grown up in the area and worked for Doc Hicks at both his home and the clinic. Winnie Payne knew the Hicks family well and still kept in touch with Margaret. In fact, she let Margaret know I was stopping in before I arrived.

When I met her, Winnie lived in a tiny apartment that sat almost on top of the railroad tracks on the Tennessee side in Copperhill. Winnie was well respected in the area and was considered a legitimate town historian. I had been warned off of others who claimed to know a thing or two about Hicks, but Frank let me know in advance who was worth my time and effort.

Winnie's apartment was more like a closet with three rooms inside, and we sat hunched in the main room, getting acquainted, during my visit. The place was built with the same blond brick as the Hicks Clinic. Winnie had opened the door to me for only one reason: Frank had told her about me and asked her to help if she could. We sat and she told me all about the area. We discussed the fire at the Ducktown Railroad Depot and how it had burned to the ground. She spoke of Cherokee Indian chiefs that towns in the area were named for. She talked about the flooding and how the river took out a lot of the businesses in town and ruined people's lives. She even spoke of the parade of not-so-legitimate sheriffs who came through McCaysville and Copperhill over the years and a crooked McCaysville mayor who spent the town's money as well.

At the young age of eighty-plus years old (she wouldn't confess her exact age), Winnie's eyes still sparkled. She knew local history in fine details, and we talked for hours. She was bright and sharp, still playing piano at local concerts and writing and preserving as much history of the town as she could for future generations. As we chatted, she gave me even more details about the river flooding that set the families of the twin cities back every time it struck and how the people would dig themselves out and start fresh again. She talked of the copper mines and the miners and how they made the area what it is today.

I told her about my visit to meet Margaret in North Carolina and how I briefly met Margaret's son at the door. She smiled and then nodded and asked for my birth date. I gave her both mine and Michelle's in case there was a roster tucked away somewhere that I didn't know about.

I was still holding on to my dream of finding a pretty box of records with a satin bow, and Frank told me if there were records, Winnie would know where they were. As we sat in her tiny living space, the older woman pulled out a notebook and wrote the dates down with our names next to each. She looked at them for a few minutes as though she was trying to remember something. Then she started to share about her work at the Hicks Clinic. She had been a receptionist on some days and would clean the clinic on others. And yet sometimes she also served as the nurse. She worked at Doc Hicks's house in Copperhill but never mentioned if she had been to or worked at his farmhouse on the Georgia side. Winnie spoke respectfully and deliberately about her work and her experiences with the Hicks family. She didn't judge them good or bad; she only spoke of what she saw and did, but her body language spoke louder than her words. She avoided my gaze when I asked her if she ever saw any of the birth mothers or the adoptive mothers coming to get the babies. But she was looking at me when I asked her about a married couple Frank had mentioned. They had gone to Doc Hicks to have their baby delivered, but it had died. When I finished laying out the question, she said nothing.

There was no more room for direct answers in this conversation, that was clear. Her face twitched, and she unconsciously adjusted her jaw as she looked away. It felt like she wanted to tell me something but couldn't. I could see that she was tired now. "I worked long hours at the clinic, sometimes not leaving there for a couple days at a time, depending on what was going on and what needed to be done. I did what I had to do." She paused and readjusted her jaw again before adding, "Anything else I can answer that you may need to know?"

I smiled through the sadness of her discomfort and what seemed to be deep sorrow, shook my head, thanked her for her time, and told her I'd see her again soon.

I called Frank as soon as I could to tell him what had transpired and all that Winnie had told me. He was quiet for a moment before asking if she had filled in the story about the married couple. I told him she hadn't. He gave me a long breathy *humph*. Waiting for more guidance, I molded my ear to the phone as he began telling a story. I sat there, once again mesmerized as he spoke. It was as if I was watching a movie. Frank said word had gotten out about Hicks somehow. Maybe directly from those involved, in their anger and desperation. Or maybe through someone in town who saw what went on just outside the doors of the clinic and put two and two together. Or maybe it was through the town sharing dirty laundry among themselves. I listened intently through the phone for some laundry to be hung.

MAGGIE AND LOUIS

The blue steel of the gun barrel almost kissed him as he sat behind his desk. It was too early in the morning to have to deal with this, although it was good that no one else was in the building besides his nurse. The hard steps echoing as they moved down the hall should have warned him of the confrontation he was about to be a part of, but they were not the first set of angry footsteps to find Hicks. This not the first person to despise him. By the time the steps reached the door to his office, it was too late to duck out the back.

Now the two men faced each other with just a few feet between them, each on one side of the desk. Nervously looking between the tip of the barrel and the man holding it, Hicks wasn't sure of his next move. It was better to be quiet. The man was sweaty; his calloused hands clenched the metal as he determined to get an answer. "Where's my wife? Where's Maggie?" The words were pushed out by the man's anger, and they reached the doctor in a slap. Hicks just stood there.

Louis had been waiting all night to see his wife and the baby she was about to deliver. They had planned to go to their family doctor when Maggie was ready, but labor had come too quick and Doc Hicks was the only nearby alternative. They had grown up knowing of Doc Hicks. The older, white-haired doctor with the boyish, round face didn't seem like such a gamble at the time or even when Hicks first told Louis that his wife needed her rest and privacy. That was before trust wore thin and what Doc Hicks referred to as Maggie's "rest" turned into hours of avoidance. Louis had had enough and was beyond playing nice.

The clinic's waiting area was a small, square room at the front of the building, positioned so the end wall was almost all window from floor to ceiling. Louis had sat in a metal card table chair facing the outside, watching throughout the night as the stars passed over the sky. He and Maggie had spent many nights watching the stars and guessing what their lives would be like with a baby, discussing names and whether the child would have his blue eyes or Maggie's brown.

He had heard her screams the evening before and went to be with her but had been told to wait. Hicks left the clinic in the evening, and Louis was told again to leave Maggie alone for a while. He tried to see his wife a few more times, but the nurse kept the door closed to the back part of the clinic, barring entry to the room where Maggie was being attended to. Almost twelve hours later, just before the sun came up, Louis could stand no more and went to get help. When he returned with his shotgun, Doc Hicks was back in his office drinking his morning coffee.

He barely had time to stand up as Louis entered the doctor's office and thrust the cool steel against his skin. "Just relax, Louis," he said. "You know I'll take good care of your wife. Just put the gun down."

"Where's Maggie? Where are she and the baby?"

"Now you know where she's at, Louis. She's in the room down the hall. I'll get my nurse to help you into the waiting room."

"No, I've had enough waiting. I want to see her now." He shoved the metal into the doctor's chest, leaving no question of his intentions. "Where's the baby? I hear crying."

––––––––––––

The doctor bit his lower lip as though sizing up how well the next story he should tell would be believed. After a long once-over of Louis, he shifted behind the desk and pretended to be sympathetic. "Your baby didn't make it. That was someone else's baby you heard. We have babies here all the time. I'm sorry for your loss."

Louis didn't move. The doctor noticed only a slight wincing before the man pushed further. "Take me to her now. Right now. Or I'll blow you into the dirt."

Hicks knew desperation, he had seen it before. The man was telling him how it would be, there was no doubt about that. Hicks raised his hands in mock surrender. Louis raked the barrel of the shotgun across his chest and around his back as the doctor slowly began moving toward the door and into the hallway. The shotgun left a mark across his freshly starched shirt. Louis was letting the doctor know he meant business. The two men shuffled down the hallway together. The doctor stopped then turned to look Louis in the face before opening the door to the room.

––––––––––––

"She's in here," Hicks told Louis. "She should be just fine. Unless, of course, something has happened that is out of my control. You know how childbirth is; it's a tricky thing. Sometimes it's just the luck of the draw." Louis stared in disgust as the doctor spoke, his cover-up almost mocking.

Hicks stepped inside and motioned for Louis to follow. The darkness blinded Louis until his eyes adjusted. The only illumination in the room came from a side lamp that gave off a dim stream of light against the closed shades and pink-tiled walls. They silhouetted the profile of a woman laid out on a surgical table. The doctor left the overhead lights off. His mumbled, incomprehensible words left Louis to decipher the meaning of what was in front of him.

Using his free hand to wipe his eyes and squinting to focus, he began to see his wife in the shadows. "Jesus! Jesus! God! What have you done to her? Turn the lights on! Turn them on! Turn them on now!"

The nurse heard the shouting from down the hall and ran to the room, flipping the switch on as she entered, startling the two men inside.

Louis froze as it hit him. The realization of the sight before him was beyond anything he could have imagined. His wife was covered in blood from the waist down. The sheet clinging to her was sopped in the reddish-brown liquid as if someone had dumped buckets upon her. The stench told the story all too well. Puddles had formed on the floor under the table, and there were bloody handprints and smudges on her face and chest where she had been unconsciously touching herself, her hands stained from searching for something, from feeling pain.

She must have been bleeding all night. The color was drained away from her once-lively face, and her body was limp and lifeless. The nurse quietly stood there, stone-faced, as Louis took it all in. She turned and closed the door behind her as Doc Hicks began to mumble about how he had tried to fix Maggie.

Louis caught himself before losing his footing, light-headed and stinging from the jolt. He lowered the shotgun to a chair against the wall and went to his wife. Bending over her, he kissed her forehead and wiped the blood off her cheek, wondering how his young, beautiful wife could be dead so soon. His tears streamed above her, falling into her hair and onto her face. The past year and a half of their courtship and marriage rushed through his mind and grief flooded him. Louis stood over her, wishing her alive again. He brushed the hair off her forehead. Her mouth opened and a faint puff of air came through her lips. For a brief second, he thought he could feel her breath. "She's not dead! Get over here and help me."

Louis looked over at Hicks for help. Head down and eyes searching for the door, Hicks was looking for an escape. Amazed at the doctor's response, Louis jumped back from the table and moved toward the exit, blocking it as the doctor tried to leave.

"Where are you going? Didn't you hear me? She's alive. Help her or I'll kill you!"

The doctor just stared at the wall as he spoke. "She's not alive; you're just grieving your loss. Let's leave her in peace."

Stupefied by the absurdity of the situation and the audacity of Hicks, Louis turned back to his wife and began removing the sheet to take her to get help. Both Hicks and the nurse tried to steer Louis away from his wife, pulling on his arms and attempting to block his way. But they paid no attention to the woman lying there. Now Louis understood even more. He broke free from the feeble couple and turned to grab his shotgun once more, leveling it at the doctor, moving him around the room with the threat of its aim. The nurse followed suit, rushing around the room and trying to be mindful of the puddles.

"I'm taking my wife and getting her some help and you're not going to stop me. Where's my baby?!" Silence. Neither the doctor nor the nurse dared say a word. He screamed at them again. "Did you hear me? Where's the baby?!"

Finally, looking to the bloodied floor and trembling, the doctor replied, "I told you, your baby died."

Louis looked to his wife and knew he had to move fast if she had a chance to live. Not wanting to leave without both his wife and child, he was in a position no man wanted, so he did what he could. "I'm going to take my wife and then I'll be back for the baby. And the baby had better be okay, or I'll kill you."

Picking up the tiny frame of the woman from the table and juggling the shotgun as his whole body shook with the combined effects of fear and anger, he moved as steadily as he could. Slowing to look one last time at the doctor and the nurse as they huddled together in the corner of the room, his burning hatred and fury vanquished their protests and pushed them into submission. He opened the door of the room and found his way to the front of the clinic.

Louis kicked open the door, dropping the shotgun as he headed toward his truck, blood dripping into the dirt and rocks of the street. Maggie's half-naked body caused some alarm among folks in the town that morning, but most were used to associating blood with the doctor and his clinic, so no one tried to help. Louis placed Maggie's body across the front seat with her head in his lap and drove furiously to the hospital in Chattanooga. He ran the truck up onto the sidewalk in his panic to get her as close to help as he could. She lost more blood on the two-hour drive from McCaysville to Chattanooga and was almost gone when they arrived. The doctor there, Reid Brown, just nodded as he looked her over and started a blood line.

Doctor Brown guessed where she had come from. Maggie wasn't the first patient he had seen from the clinic in McCaysville, and he was more than familiar with the carnage of botched procedures. When Louis tried to explain about Hicks and how he had butchered his wife, leaving her to die, Brown said nothing except that it would be a good thing for him to make funeral arrangements. Louis hung his head.

———————

Doctor Brown sat in his office, not sure of what to do next. He would try to save the woman, of course. Thomas J. Hicks had first been his mentor and later his father-in-law when he'd married Hicks's daughter, Margaret. Now Hicks was a loose cannon. He had sent women out of his clinic too ripped and torn for anyone with even the worst of morals to ignore. Reid Brown had learned basic family practice from Hicks at the McCaysville clinic in the early days of his career, and now he was seeing the effects of age, greed, and disease as they crept up on the older doctor.

———————

Doc Hicks's voice was clear and direct as it came across the phone lines after being connected by the switchboard operator. "Just come down and get it. It'll be healthy. Bring a check with you or get one when you get down here if you don't have cash on hand. Mabel, you can disconnect us now." And then his voice was gone.

The couple's car was packed and ready to go two hours later, and they began the fifteen-hour drive south to Georgia to collect a baby. They drove all night from Ohio and were tired and hungry. Hicks had told the couple that he had a baby for them, although he wasn't sure whether it was a boy or a girl. They'd know more in the morning.

Hicks smiled at the couple from Ohio who were now sitting at his desk and told them about the newborn baby he had waiting for them in the next room. And, Hicks told them, he wasn't too expensive either.

———————

Louis sat next to his wife in the hospital, watching her whenever he could slip away from work, hoping she would wake. Days slipped into weeks and then months as Maggie slept. She lay in the bed, clean and peaceful. Louis forgot about the shotgun he had dropped outside of the Hicks Clinic. He tried to forget about the baby too. Almost three months after giving birth, Maggie woke up from her coma and asked to see her child. The one with the brown eyes.

Frank finished that story and added a few more references from his experience and accounts of friends and past coworkers. He outlined how the Hicks Clinic would be shut up tight with the doors locked, shades down, and lights off when the ambulance he drove pulled up in front in response to a call for an emergency pickup. They'd arrive to find a girl on the curb clutching herself, arms wrapped tightly around her body as she sat bleeding and in pain, tears streaming down her face and fearing for her life. They'd pick her up and take her to a hospital to get proper care.

"It was a sad sight to see, but what could we do other than take care of the girls?" Frank sounded both disgusted and calm at the same time. "But I saw who he was, that's for sure. And those of us in town that saw it took note."

"Did anyone say something to law enforcement? Was there anything done?" I asked.

Frank was quick to respond. "Law enforcement was very standoffish. There were a lot of politics going on that were dangerous to be involved in for everyone. Some things that happened in McCaysville weren't always clear or easily understood, and if you fought them, it could be pretty bad."

Frank told me more about the countless families in McCaysville and Copperhill who swore their babies had been born alive and yet lost them to the Hicks Clinic and the doctor who told them they were hearing things and they were crazy. He shared about the mistresses in town, one a beauty shop owner, who put the pregnant girls to work sweeping floors and cleaning up after clients right up until they had their own babies in order to work off their debt to Doc Hicks for his services. Services that included the birth procedures and boarding in one of the tiny one-room apartments attached to the Hicks Clinic, as if giving him their baby wasn't enough. And he relayed several incidents of drug addictions to opiates fueled by Hicks because of his tendency to enjoy the finances of repeat customers. Frank confirmed the indictment story and gave me a few details that he knew about some of the people who sat on the jury and what he knew about the horror of the situation. I couldn't take notes fast enough and was anxious over missing something until Frank brought it all back around to what was most important by asking, "But all these stories aren't what you need now, are they?" There was quiet for a few awkward moments before he continued. "Winnie didn't give you any information about a possible birth mother?"

Frank sensed my tears when I didn't respond and gave me an out. I could tell he was trying to be lighter, a little more cheerful. Like a father to his daughter when she falls off her bike and scrapes her knee, who then gently prods her to keep trying. "You've had another long day! Feel free to call me back if you need more help. I'll help if I can." With a thank-you and an acknowledgment of his promise, I was on my way back to the cemetery to catch the sunset and debrief for the day.

NINE

1997

URING MY CHILDHOOD and into my early teens, I hung around the garage of my father's long-haul trucking business. Mostly I would spend my time irritating the mechanics, but on some days, they'd let me drive one of the cars used to run parts all over the dirty parking lot and back around the concrete-block garage. My favorite car was an old beat-up 1960s blue-and-chalky-white Suburban that, on an exemplary day, would make it over forty mph and on other days was lucky if it started. It gave its passengers a bumpy, lurching ride with a good share of shaking and staggering. The blue was painted on by hand and was so bright that it glowed against the white. The tires were like big balloons, and it had a horn that stuck and sounded like a high-pitched auctioneer prattling on and on. I had to hit the dash over and over until the mechanism caught and brought back silence. I called her Big Blue, and she accompanied me on several high school evenings with friends as we bounced our way across Akron, making mischief now best forgotten.

Memories of the truck yard came up at a pivotal moment in my life, when the challenges were clear, and the memory cheered me on to keep going. I shook my head free of Big Blue and returned to the business at hand. Back in Georgia, I was standing at the bottom of the steps of the Fannin County Courthouse once again. I'd come to a point in my search where I felt just like that old Suburban, trying to get the show on the road but not sure if I was ever going anywhere. With my sights set on the probate office, I could hear that old Suburban rattling its metal and its engine humming as I walked across the threshold again with birth certificate in hand.

Two beautiful and smiling women greeted me, once again making the Fannin County Probate Court the friendliest government agency, state or federal, in which I'd pulled reports or certificates. And once again, I told my story and the basics of what I knew about the Hicks Clinic. I had the birth certificate I'd memorized since childhood in my bag but wanted to see what could be found, if there was more or even different info. I left that building grateful for the respect I received during my visit, and within a couple of days, I was back in Ohio planning my next steps. I communicated with the courthouse several times after that visit. Eventually I realized it was time to go public with the story in hopes of finding more people like me, to bring as many of us together as possible to find records or birth mothers.

I knew there were others. Michelle and my cousin Markie were proof. And faint whispers of a few other children our pediatrician took care of led me to believe they were also from the

Hicks Clinic. But my heart all but stopped when I learned through my research that over two hundred babies were sold at the clinic. My mind wrestled with the number. I had thought there were maybe twenty or thirty. I knew then what I had to do clear as day. I hung up the phone with the courthouse and picked it right back up, waiting for the dial tone so I could call a journalist with a local paper in Akron and beg for a couple lines in her column.

The journalist listened to my story and asked me what proof I had. I gave her more details and the number for the courthouse. A week went by and she called, this time more attentive, asking more questions. I assumed then she would include my small plea to connect me with other Hicks Babies and I would soon have a group to work with, an army of sorts to conquer the mystery of McCaysville and the Hicks Clinic. We had a few more conversations and then she told me they were going to run a story. But she was sure it would be small and buried in the lifestyle section. She promised to get the information that I had requested out and said they wanted to take pictures for the story. Michelle and I had our pictures taken at my house and we thought little about it. That's how naive we were.

Everyone thinks it's glamorous being in news articles and on TV, but it's not. It may be for professionals and celebrities, but not for those in news flashes, those of us who have normal lives. The story hit the front page of the *Akron Beacon Journal* and the *AP Wire* the morning of Mother's Day 1997, and it was my last morning of calm for some time as the story of the Hicks Babies was let loose. It caught the attention of Akronites who were born in Georgia, and phone calls started pouring in from people with Hicks Clinic birth certificates.

Many had been lied to their whole lives, not knowing they were adopted, so a lot of explaining was needed to fill them in on the Hicks Clinic. My heart broke knowing that soon they would be aware of the deeper, personal meaning of what *sold* and *bought* meant. Calls and letters barraged me to the tune of three-hundred-plus a day in a pre-internet frenzy. People were asking questions and throwing information at me rapid-fire, hoping to connect their truth to mine. Many were not related to the Hicks Clinic. Some mothers who had given up a baby or lost one grasped at restoration. McCaysville townsfolk felt a need to call and defend the town and the good doctor like they had fought to keep the secrets nearly a decade after I first slipped into town to ask questions.

Just under fifty babies from the Hicks Clinic came forward when the article was published. Some wanted to stay anonymous, and that was honored. Soon after, a steady number of them, at first separately, found themselves sitting on the couch in my living room with birth certificates in hand. Some cried and asked questions, others were quiet and stared out the picture window as I shared the overview of what I knew. A few were angry while others broke down in frustration and confusion. Some were relieved and eager to know more.

It wasn't long before the majority were together in my backyard as familiar strangers. Grown adults looked one another up and down to see if anything matched, hoping to find clues to the unknown. Red hair, green eyes, pale skin, tall or robust, brown eyes, blonde or black hair, short or skinny. They came from all walks of life and social strata. There wasn't one common thread in their looks or traits. They told their stories and what they knew and tried to listen to the facts, but sometimes it was too much to take in. Most looked overwhelmed and, if they hadn't been told about their adoption before, by the time they came together with the others, they knew the stark truth of it all.

I was born in 1965. Over thirty years later, I stood looking out from my back door at others who were sold at birth by the same doctor to couples in Akron, just like my parents. I questioned what is harder, the thought of being sold or finding out why I was sold. The glass doors separated me from the strangers, with the exception of Michelle, who was sitting on my back patio. I could see the stress across the strangers' faces. They had come together only because of the story in the local newspaper two weeks earlier. Some had traveled from out of state to meet but most were from Akron. They sat waiting for guidance from me, and I stood there hoping their presence would refresh my strength.

Watching them, studying their movements, seeing and feeling the tension of the crowd, a mix of pity and fear flooded my senses. Each individual sat comparing themself to the person sitting beside them, as though hoping for the possibility of finding a sister or brother. Their desire and curiosity seemed to override any doubt or inhibitions. It was a bizarre circumstance, and they were strong to be there, strong just for showing up.

That day we began to share the burden given us at birth. Pink and blue bundles born out of strife, bought rather than being adopted. My entire life seemed to have worked its way up to that moment. The struggle to understand how flesh and circumstance could be brokered so easily set my course, pushing me from my early childhood, inching me toward insight. It was apparent none of us were special. Cash for a baby and a fake birth certificate. Snake oil at a circus sideshow.

When I closed my eyes, I could envision the disgusting little building that was once the Hicks Clinic, a circus of its own. It now stood empty and abused, mocking the degree of its use from the past. I could see the river racing behind it and its sun-faded bricks. The fellow adoptees sitting on my back patio drove home the singular aspect of my search I had avoided for so long and now couldn't ignore. I stood glued there, watching, taking in the emotion, suddenly overwhelmed by the responsibility of what would come next. I had searched on my own and liked the comfort of flying under the radar.

From the time the story broke, I had been too busy hassling with newspapers and television producers, selling their shows like peddlers pushing bad wares, to think of my own feelings. And right at that moment, every one of them hit me full in the face, taking me back to those years of searching in fine detail. I was still standing at the back door wrapped in the memories of the clinic and how I had gotten to this point in my search when one of the adoptees looked up and motioned to me. He lifted his plastic cup in a mock toast. "It's time to compare toes, Janie. Maybe we'll find some that match!"

Everyone laughed, and I found myself smiling at the thought. Toes, they wanted to compare toes. I hadn't thought about that. Then it struck me, and I could feel the emotion and fought it back, because I knew what a monster Hicks was. I'd heard the stories and I didn't want these babies to know. Not right now. They had toes to compare.

TEN

Where the Babies Went

COMPARING TOES should make everyone smile. We are all human, are we not? At some time in life, every questioning soul is wrapped up in the color of their eyes, the wave in their hair, or where those attributes came from and why. Family traits, like the story of Grandpa and his long nose or Cousin Thelma's tiny ears and how those traits were shared through the genetic line over the years, are like a meandering stream running across and then depositing DNA upon the generations. Small things defining what is whole. That first group meetup of possible Hicks Babies blossomed into an opportunity, a possibility of finding someone not known to exist, someone never thought of before. It quickly became the possibility to redeem time lost.

Having spent enough time observing behind the glass doors, I steeled myself to join the group, and as I stepped outside, one of the Hicks Babies, a man named Paul, raised his cup, making a toast that everyone joined in.

Paul Reymann was a relaxed and kind man. I could tell that from the start. The day after the story ran in the *Akron Beacon Journal*, he called and asked me if what was published was true—that he could be a Hicks Baby. He grew up knowing he was adopted but wasn't told his parents got him through a stolen-baby transaction. Paul had a Hicks Clinic birth certificate but not much more to go on. When he saw the front-page story on Mother's Day, he was devastated and confronted his father, demanding the truth. His adoptive mother had passed when he was only eleven, and as far as his father was concerned, the secret was buried with her. So Paul grew up not knowing the details of his adoption and never questioning his origins. That is, until he saw the *Akron Beacon Journal* article that gave him a good reason to question it.

Paul and I talked on the phone and discussed the Hicks Clinic a couple times after the article came out, but he came to my house for the first time the afternoon of the get-together. He boldly admitted to everyone that he wasn't sure what he wanted or was getting into but quickly threw in his support for the rest of us. On that day, his only desire was to let any birth mothers know how thankful he was to them for coming forward. And that's how I wanted it to start. Everyone had their own journey to take and their own time line. My heart was to give them a vehicle to get where they wanted, where they needed to go.

Many of those who gathered with us were in the dark about Doc Hicks and didn't know the details of their birth story or even that they were adopted. Mark Eckenrode sat on the patio that day with his wife, Georgeanne. Mark was fair-haired and blue-eyed, and I immediately earmarked him as a possible heir to Doc Hicks himself since I had heard the McCaysville folk tell of Hicks and his mistresses. Mark and Paul bantered back and forth about shared traits of the group and kept us laughing. They both shared a semitwisted sense of humor.

Mark had called a couple days after the story broke and asked to meet with me. He was confused because he had a Hicks Clinic birth certificate but wasn't adopted. He'd asked his mother, and she denied any secrets. Before he hung up the phone on our first conversation, he quietly, almost whispering, asked me if I thought he was a Hicks Baby. I told him to come to the house so we could discuss it further but to ask his mother again. By the time he and I finished talking that day, I knew he was a Hicks Baby. His story was too similar to the others I was hearing.

The next day Mark was standing on my front porch with birth certificate in hand, all but waving it like a flag in a July Fourth parade. I could see the fatigue on his face. His beautiful wife was with him, and she smiled and tried to keep it light while supporting her husband, knowing his hurt. The three of us sat for a couple hours, working through the details of his birth and the story he was given as a child. His mother and father had been vacationing in Florida, and on the return drive home, while running through McCaysville, she went into labor and stopped at the Hicks Clinic. That was what he had been told. He sat on my couch in disbelief, the look on his face told more than any words could have fleshed out the lie. The first time he asked his mother about it, she stood by her story, claiming she had given birth to him.

Fighting for his newly found truth, that day he went home and confronted his mother again, presenting her with the details of the Hicks Clinic I'd given him. She broke down and finally told him the truth. Mark was back at my home within days, and we were going over more details, some from his mother. His father had never mentioned anything before his death years before. Mark was a seasoned genealogist and had worked for over a decade to extensively map out his Eckenrode family tree. Now it all seemed a waste of his time. He had nothing to start over with, only a fake birth certificate. Mark quickly became engaged in the search for birth mothers.

On that first day, the first gathering at my house, Mark unexpectedly connected with some childhood friends. He walked into the backyard to find several others he knew growing up. Such a small world, as the parents had kept up a friendship with their main connection to the Hicks Clinic, a woman who had, for lack of a better term, brokered the transactions for the babies. Not fathoming that one day the kids would find the truth—that the adoptive parents had created a small, social circle of Hicks Clinic babies. But together they sat in my backyard telling the stories and details of their lives based upon the circumstances of the Hicks Clinic.

They shared stories of their childhood summers spent on the banks of Lake Erie at friends and family gatherings and how the years of shared summers ran steadily into their teens. The excitement of reconnecting was fun to watch and was as it should have been. They were all smiles as they chatted away; it was a good thing to see.

One of the quiet ones was Diane. She had traveled from Michigan—one of the few to grow up outside of Akron. With dark hair and a petite frame, she was perfectly put together and watched the rest of us as we compared tales of growing up in

Ohio. Akron was a different world for her, and this was already shaping up to be a hard crowd to break into with the uncharted territory we were all wading through. She had recently begun looking for her birth information, and the timing couldn't have been better. Knowing she was adopted from the Hicks Clinic, Diane wanted more information to fill in the blanks of her story. Her adoptive mother loved her and was open and truthful about the details of getting Diane as a newborn. She had worked hard to give her a good life, but the desire to know more burned in Diane.

Several of those who gathered didn't want to have their names published or to participate in the news pieces, and that was understandable. I listened to what the majority wanted and weighed that against what I already knew, wanted to know, and thought could be done. After consulting with a few DNA labs and an attorney or two, a DNA registry was set up and I chose to allow information to pass as a two-way mirror for anyone wanting their information but not wanting to meet or be unmasked.

I made my parameters clear to everyone in the group. Choices were few and far between in North Georgia in the forties, fifties, and sixties, and women had been mistreated for their connection to the Hicks Clinic. It was my goal to give the birth mothers the respect they deserved. My intent to protect them over anyone else was made clear then and remains clear to this day. Not everyone in the group was on the same page, and some wanted to expose the birth mothers. I make no apologies for my decisions.

As the Akron group began to form, even more people with Hicks Clinic birth certificates from Georgia, Tennessee, and the

Carolinas came forward asking for help. Some had grown up right in Copperhill or McCaysville. There were angry adoptees from both the North and the South.

One story that stood out was that of Stephen. Remembering the first phone call from him still saddens me. What I could make of his story of childhood abuse and abandonment was clearly painful, but it was hard to determine what I could do for him. We talked several times over a few weeks and his struggle was palpable, but I worried a sibling or birth mother might react if I connected them. The details he shared with me sat heavy on my heart. He was wounded and the only help I could offer was referring him to run his DNA through our registry. There was no match in 1997, and years went by before I heard directly from Stephen again. His search continued with his daughter's help.

Several others had similar childhood experiences and still others had perfect scenarios of growing up just a stone's throw from the clinic. The disparity of placement of babies with families who either abused and neglected their children and the parents who cherished the babies they got from Hicks was amazing to me. Where was the safety net for us? If Doctor Hicks had set up a system to check on the babies he placed, with the exception of the stolen babies, most of the adoptions wouldn't have been a mere transaction, they would have been legal. I began to wrap my head around that and ended up shaking it more in disbelief than in understanding.

Every time I thought I had gathered my bearings, the story took off on a tangent like the biggest fish you've ever seen on a deep-sea expedition. I found myself conducting more damage control due to misinformation to protect myself and others than connecting with people. It was important to get the story out to find birth mothers, but the truth was getting lost in the ghost of Doctor Hicks. And my, how it took off. It was covered by every media outlet from local television and radio stations to the major networks like CNN, ABC, NBC, CBS, Fox News, and daytime talk shows to the *New York Times*, *USA Today*, and *People* magazine. The story was out, the group I had wanted was forming, the media loved and at the same time distorted the story, and the town of McCaysville was understandably indignant.

Like watching a pile of leaves with smoke pouring from it, I sat and waited to see if it would catch fire. With my experience in adoption search and in my personal search, I've interviewed many adoptees, adoptive parents, and birth mothers, so I've seen a thing or two. Some of those searching wonder how much money their birth mother has and want an explanation as to who she thought she was to give them up. These people were asking me—no, expecting me—to help them find their birth mother, as though they were entitled to that knowledge. I'd sit back for a few minutes and take a deep breath to settle myself down before responding.

The majority just wanted to find their birth family. Most of the people connected to the Hicks Clinic were eager to join our group and were curious about what they would find. Through the DNA registry we set up, reunions began between Hicks Babies and birth families, returning what was stolen.

My search had been private most of my life, just fragments shared with my sister and a few friends. It had become almost sacred to me. The research and connections I made were like the fine gold and jewels on a crown. I protected my work and the privacy of my sources for so long and wasn't about to hand everything over to someone who might not see its worth. One wrong move and birth mothers would be scattered. Worse, birth mothers would hide and feel more condemnation than had already been heaped upon them by the doctor and their circumstances. These women were worth fighting for just as much as finding the truth of our births. Both were important and both were sorely needed, and striking a balance meant finding a way back to running leads to help both. It meant getting out of the circus the media had helped create.

I felt like everything I had worked for was beginning to unravel and might fall apart if I wasn't careful. Lacking prior experience with the media, I felt bruised and defeated. So I dug in again and concentrated on my comfort zone, investigating and running leads.

Frank called to congratulate me, laughing as he did. "Well, you sure opened a big can of worms with this one." His tone was lighthearted, and I couldn't help but smile in agreement. Talking with him was a nice reprieve from the media deluge, and it was good to hear a friendly voice from McCaysville. If there's a way to hear someone smile through a phone call, it was at that moment when he said, "You did good, girl. You did good. Proud to have helped ya. Just be careful."

"Thank you. That means the world." It was good to hear his voice. Memories of the florist shop and the kindness he showed me, as well as the wonderful aroma of the flowers, flooded through me. That was the last time I spoke with Frank. I've always regretted not talking to him more before he passed, but I was overwhelmed and time got away from me as the story took on a life of its own.

Whenever anyone asks me about what it was like to walk around McCaysville back in the beginning of my search, I think of Frank, his warmth, and his willingness to share what he knew and take a calculated risk on a young woman who walked into his shop one day. He was a gift to me, and I can only take comfort hoping that he heard me smiling back at him through the phone that day. *You did good, girl. You did good.*

ELEVEN

Just Past Nicholson's

IN FOURTEEN YEARS OF SEARCHING, I had uncovered a fair share of colorful stories about Hicks and had discussions with birth mothers, some Fannin County officials, and townsfolk from McCaysville. But all of that left me short on hard evidence connected to my own birth mother. I don't recommend trusting and indulging a newspaper with highly personal information but, having exhausted all other avenues and with the technology being what it was at the time, I felt I had no other choice.

The news of stolen babies traveled fast from Akron to the North Georgia region, and my face was plastered on television and the front pages of newspapers for months. Immediately, my search moved south almost full time, and for quite a while after my story broke, cameras and hounding reporters followed my search from a close distance. That was when I learned how much I like my privacy. When the search became public knowledge, leads began pouring in. Many were offering up innocent women who had given up babies at Doc Hicks's clinic, but this did me no good if the women themselves weren't coming forward. A few months into running with the leads I'd received, I took a call about a woman who looked just like me and had given up a baby or two at the local clinic. She said the woman had given birth to a girl in January of 1965.

Sitting at the desk in my hotel room, I listened carefully to the hundredth person tell me she was or knew my birth mother. Many women called to parrot my vital statistics, since they had been given out by the newspapers, hoping to convince me of a connection between the two of us. As with those other calls, I closed my eyes, waiting for my sense of investigation to kick in and override my cynicism. I jotted down the pertinent information, trying to make sense of the instructions, as she calmly dictated directions to her home in Turtletown.

"C'mon out to the house," she told me. "Follow Route 68 north past Nicholson's grocery, and then it's six-tenths of a mile to the green house where you'll make a left. There's no street sign. Follow that to the fork in the road and go right. My house is the blue one at the end of the street. It's a ways up the mountain." The woman finished giving me directions and then added one more thing. "Oh, and her name was Kitty." *Was.* That word stuck with me. And then the voice was gone, and I was left with a piece of paper with scrawled notations.

Because I was too busy with leads and everything going on around me, it was a couple days before I went to meet the lady I'd talked to on the phone, following the instructions to a T to avoid getting lost.

Pulling into the driveway and cautiously getting out, I walked to the porch and climbed the steps. The porch was nice enough, swept clean and filled with white wicker furniture. As I was moving across the porch, I didn't recognize at the time that I was walking into the moment I had waited for all of my life. The striving and searching were coming to an end.

The front door opened and a woman named Carlynn, who I knew only from the phone call, stood in its frame looking at me. She said nothing, obviously shocked by my appearance. She leaned against the door, the door being the only thing keeping her standing. Slowly and methodically she spoke. "I knew you looked like her, but I didn't expect you to look exactly like her."

Like the six-year-old me who couldn't comprehend *black market*, I was in the smoke-clouded past. I needed time to adjust to her statement. We were both silent, standing at the door. She was having a hard time looking at my too-familiar features, but I was looking her full in the face, challenging one more person to lie to me. A few moments later she moved away from the door and asked me in. We sat at her dining room table and I listened as she spoke, fighting the sense of being overwhelmed.

I never thought the blueprint of finding my birth mother would include what I was being told, so I didn't catch everything Carlynn had to say right then. She told me Kitty had passed ten years before. That night I laid in bed at the hotel, fragments of the conversation filling my head, making stabs at my heart and telling me that, finally, maybe I was someone's daughter.

Two days after the meeting with Carlynn, I found myself fumbling with my jotted notes, following the instructions to the house once again. Drawn back to it to learn more, I stood on the porch in front of the closed door, lost in thought about why I was there. It was then that I realized Carlynn could see right through me and had from the start.

I startled and looked up to find the door wide open. She smiled and moved back, motioning for me to come inside. We discussed almost everything about Kitty for hours, and when I got up to leave, Carlynn took both my hands in hers and held them tight. "You're welcome here, just like Kitty was. Come back, stay awhile and rest, and find a piece of quiet when you can. You need rest. It's time to rest, and my home is yours. I consider you a part of my family as well. She would want that." The words rang loud, but I struggled with the emotion of their meaning and the sincerity in which they were given.

It had been so long since anyone had been family, too long since someone told me it was okay to lay down my sword and stop fighting. Her offer came right in the middle of my chaos and she knew it. She reassured me and told me to trust her and when I was ready, we would both explore Kitty's life together, if that was what I wanted. It wasn't long before I was spending as much of my time as I could at Carlynn's home, wrestling with the media that were still on my back, dealing with them before I could find the peace to trust a stranger and learn about my birth mother. That wise and loving woman patiently waited for me to catch up to Kitty as I began to surrender, piece by piece, to the stillness and the quiet.

I didn't have much to say. It was seven thirty in the morning and most of the time I don't breathe that early, let alone talk. First thing I did after my feet hit the floor was wrap myself in the quilt from the bed, shuffle to the front porch at Carlynn's house, and make a beeline for the wicker love seat, almost falling into it. Snuggled up in the quilt, I was oblivious to everything around me as I waited for the sun's warmth to arrive, hoping the haze in my head would clear soon.

Carlynn joined me, sitting in the chair with one leg up, flat-footed on the seat. She was smoking a cigarette and chuckling at the look of me, like she did every morning.

The house phone rang, and she got up, leaving me alone and numb on the porch, until minutes later when she poked her head back out the door. The grin on her face told me she was still amused by the way that I looked. Throw into the picture my yellow cotton little boys' pajamas. I was most definitely a sight.

"You haven't eaten breakfast," she said. "How about some tea?" Her Southern drawl interrupted my state of mind.

Her lips curled upward as I cleared my throat and stammered back at her, "I'd love some, thanks." After my reply she was gone again and sounds began to purr in the kitchen.

My eyes shut automatically as I settled back into an almost comatose state, the quilt tightly enveloping me. Sitting on the porch always made me lazy and dreamy. It was a place for dreaming. Right in the middle of what seemed like nowhere, the sounds and smells of the countryside could easily overwhelm and seduce even the most citified person. No one could resist the huge trees; no streetlights or power cables distracted attention from them or the endless blue sky that encircled the mountain. Pine and fresh flowers could not be ignored or masked by clouds of diesel from the few trucks that wound their way up and down the mountainside. Every so often a car horn could be heard screaming at a cow or dog in the road, but the noise was drowned out quickly by quiet as the animal lumbered away at a slow, steady pace.

The roads are mostly dirt and gravel, and that's all right. No one complains; it is typical. A solitary cut in the trees snakes its way from the main throughway between small hills and takes you to Carlynn's front yard, just a short ride off of the Tennessee side of McCaysville. About ten acres of mowed grass, the yard is framed by old trees, covering rough mountain rock that began as family territory. The mountain had been staked by her great-great-grandfather Blalock years ago and is thought to be the most beautiful land in the Tennessee Smokies. It was a good, peaceful place to have as home.

Carlynn's house was always lovely, but the best thing about it was the porch. Running almost the entire length of the front of the house, it was an outdoor theater of sights and sounds and all things natural and beautiful. Plants hung from each corner, with hummingbird feeders every two feet, accommodating the flashing miniature birds. Its roof was high enough to afford a full view of the mountains, and under its roof, deep enough to hold family get-togethers in a pinch of bad weather.

Painted white, the porch was a stark contrast to the deep blue of the house and the forest greens around it, sitting in the cradle of the mountain like a baby. You could see the entire clearing while sitting there, and if you listened real close, neighbors' voices traveled across the yard, perhaps during an argument, providing entertainment on a slow day.

Coming up the road to the house, you can see it first thing and use it to gauge whether anyone is home. Rommel, Carlynn's loyal dog, would stick his big, black head out from the steps end of the porch if no one was home, sizing up visitors and giving warning that an ugly rottweiler was on duty. If you couldn't find him on guard, then he was probably cooling off under the porch in the orange clay. He thought it was his porch. Everybody thought it was their porch. In good and bad times, people gathered to share or console or just sit, pondering while they rocked or lazed. It can stand on its own for what it's worth.

I sat on that porch many times and planned days, years, and lifetimes. I mulled over what went wrong in my life and what went right. I sought answers to questions and sometimes I looked for nothing except the beauty of rest and comfort far away from the madness of my everyday life. Time and time again, I went back to that porch to sort out life and immerse myself in the peace it provided.

That morning, as I waited for Carlynn to reappear with our tea, my eyes focused and I watched the mist coming off the tops of the trees as the sun heated up the air. Finally, I began to wake up and let the quilt slip to my waist. As the air warmed, my mind revved and started wrestling with thoughts of previous morning conversations on the porch. There's something about the mix of beauty and solitude that makes past events clearer, painting them in rich, vivid colors and making them easier to digest.

The first day Carlynn and I sat together and talked about Kitty will stay with me as long as I live and beyond. When she saw me on TV, she thought she was looking at an old friend. Carlynn was a social worker who saw her clients as more than a job, and she became a friend to Kitty, as she did to me. Carlynn reached out when she realized I was Kitty's daughter, not a picture of the friend who'd passed years before. At our first meeting she told me that my birth mother was dead. Killed in a car wreck over a decade before the story broke in 1997. Carlynn's knowledge of Kitty was all I had, and she became the bridge between us.

Years of working for the Tennessee Department of Human Services had made her cautious. Mountain people and the Ku

Klux Klan filled her everyday docket of cases, forcing her to reach deep into the depths of understanding to keep from being swallowed by the harshness of life high up on the mountain. Neglected children and abused mothers made her days full and long. Many times she worked under duress created by the striving that permeates the way of life for most in the area. Carlynn spent her childhood summers there but went to school in Miami, adding to her character of toughness and intelligence.

She had traveled widely, so as she got older and wiser, she knew her Tennessee home would be a good place to settle. At sixty-two, Carlynn could put a woman half her age to shame. A slow smile on a model-perfect face, coupled with an hourglass shape atop long legs, made her a pleasant sight. Although beautiful, she transcended to the spiritual and knew how to touch broken people in order to make them better. Her strength came from God and inspired even the most hardened hearts to soften, shaming the unfortunate who have never known a woman like Carlynn.

I was staring out into the trees when Carlynn returned and handed me a cup of tea. She knew when I was stressed or worried, and she'd respond by spoiling me even more than usual. "Drink your tea and we'll talk," she quietly commanded as she sat down in her chair. Her maternal Southern roots shone through the words.

I sipped the hot liquid, and we watched the hummingbirds jockey for position around the feeders, their colors mixing and colliding in the fresh morning sun. It was good to be there. The sun filtering across the front yard and reviving the sleepy land was a perfect sight that played out every morning. Just before my cup was dry, Carlynn looked at me and smiled cautiously.

Although I didn't recognize it at the time, I know now that her expression was a mix of sadness and remembrance. "I know the papers have said a few things about Kitty and her family," she said, "but what have they told you about Kitty?"

I stirred, knowing that the tone of her voice and my own curiosity warranted my full attention. "Just that she was the oldest of nine and was married at twenty. Other than that, just gossip and hearsay. You know how people like to hear themselves talk."

Carlynn shielded her eyes from the sun and turned to take a good look at me, tilting her head off to the side slightly like she was critiquing a painting. "You look just like her, right down to the wave in her hair." With a mischievous grin she added, "Except her chest was bigger."

"Thanks, it's always nice to know when you missed a gene here or there." I rolled my eyes. "Don't tell me she was also five inches taller. That might get to me." Her grin transformed back to a sweet smile again. "I was just testing to see if you had woke up yet." We both laughed and she continued to size me up before going further. "Sometimes I see the orneriness creep up into your eyes just like it used to with Kitty. There's a spark that flashes behind the color. You have it too. I've seen it more than once." She paused for a moment. "Did I ever tell you about the time she threw bricks over the hill at the bootleggers, smashed the back windshield in, and made an unpleasant sight for those boys? Boys they were too. And she didn't want them around her home."

Her face screwed up at the thought of Kitty all mad and running after men with moonshine in the back of their car. "I'll tell you that one later. I want you to know it all, but that one is for later."

She sat back in her chair and took a slow drag off a second cigarette. "She had a temper. Most of the time she was sweet as can be, but mess with her in the wrong way or hurt anyone she loved and watch out." Carlynn chuckled at the thought and looked up to the sky as I sat waiting for more, mulling over what little I knew of my birth mother.

Carlynn didn't leave me waiting for long. She shared more information than I could have dreamed.

I learned that Kitty was just fifteen when she had me. And I was her second. Both babies were given up for adoption to a doctor who preferred cash to anything else. Kitty had no choice; she was just another pregnant girl needing her burden lifted, and Hicks was in the practice of lifting burdens. With no prenatal care or help, Kitty's mother just took her to the doc when labor started. After she entered the building alone, only those there knew what happened, and they would not tell. Her life moved forward in an unlucky sprint of events, and several years later she married an abusive man named James who made her life a nightmare. To this day no one knows why she married him. The brutality of her death is a caricature of James's evil. It didn't matter how he tormented her as long as he got what he wanted.

A tractor trailer collided with her tiny car, leaving only pieces in a heap. The lack of hard evidence left the Georgia Bureau of Investigation unable to prove foul play, although they believed her brake line had been cut. It wasn't difficult to figure out who would have cut it. James had threatened to kill her and their son more than once before. He'd even been known to light the house on fire every two or three years while they were inside.

Kitty had been returning from her mother's house after depositing the last of her and her son's clothes before making a final trip back to the house she shared with James, for the dog. Her next stop was the Fannin County Probate Court. Separation papers had been filed that morning, and by afternoon they lay dormant at the courthouse, voided by her death.

She was planning to leave him for the last time. Her life was ordinary for women in that part of the country. You're born and you live, if poverty and abuse don't kill you, and then you fade. Like colors painted in the sun, there's not much left after a while for anyone to see, only to remember.

When Carlynn introduced me around, some of Kitty's family members gave me pictures so I could see her smile and her eyes. Carlynn was right. Her auburn hair, the green-blue eyes were the same as mine, along with everything else, but I had a hard time seeing her picture without being able to touch her. The same dark auburn hair and eyes that change from green to blue and back within minutes are locked into a place somewhere.

Carlynn's voice jolted me back to the porch again. "Kitty and I, we used to sit out here for hours watching the night and talking. That's how I learned about the doctor and the babies. It wasn't until later that she pointed the clinic out to me when we were in town."

Carlynn looked away from me to mask the pain. Later she told me she and Kitty had sat outside the clinic just a few days before Kitty was killed. They talked about new beginnings and what her future would be like without James. "She loved it in the summer when the fireflies would swarm right over there under the big oak." Carlynn pointed to the tree and took another drag off her cigarette. I scrutinized the leaves and the trunk and tried to picture pinpoints of light dancing around in the cool evening air. "They were like bees, there were so many. We would sit drinking Coke and we'd talk about everything from men to horses."

She moved forward in the chair and let out a breath, almost whispering a secret that only she and I should know. "She only knew that her babies had been taken north to Ohio. She told me how, if she could just have gone there for a day and stood behind a tree or fence to watch, to see you, she would have been happy. She wanted so much for her babies. She wished for so much. She wanted the normal everyday things that most take for granted and that should have been such a small thing to wish for." Carlynn paused. "This porch became sort of a wishing well for her, sometimes in reality and sometimes in dreams. She never spoke of her babies any other time, even though I knew she was always thinking about them. Her eyes would latch on to every single little girl she saw, and she did hair at the church for the little ones on Sundays just so she could touch them. Even though it hurt her, she never complained. She never blamed anyone."

I shifted in the love seat and ran my hands through my hair, pretending to be neutral to the fact that when either of us said babies, we meant me. "Did she ever search for the babies?"

Carlynn shook her head and put it back against the top of the chair, contemplating the answer. "She didn't. Times were different then, and she had no means to look beyond this area. She knew you weren't around here. Besides, she wanted more for her babies than what you could get here. She told me she hoped her babies would get a good education and could work in a good place. She didn't want them to have her reality; she wanted so much more for her babies."

Closing my eyes, I tried to imagine Kitty watching me as a child. Would I have known? Felt her? I've always relied on not believing in would haves, could haves, or should haves, but it's tough not to ask questions. How life might have gone under different circumstances if I was ever afforded a second chance.

Eyes still closed and with only half of my voice, I whispered back to Carlynn, "It's hard trying to picture her and who she was. It's so foreign to me. I never thought it would be this hard." My hand moved upward to my face, feeling the curves, imagining another with the same features. "I've waited all my life to find her, and now . . ."

My mind raced to all the times I stood in front of a mirror and wondered who I looked like, who had my eyes. I wanted to see her. In an instant both my heart and mind converged, realizing she would never know me. She would never see me. My body slumped in the love seat, exhausted and demoralized. I was tired of guessing, imagining.

Carlynn was quiet while I played with the strings on the quilt, fumbling for a distraction. Finally, she spoke, and I began to relax and pull back from the pain. "I have some of her clothes in a box up at my mother's house. We kept them there whenever she would go back to live with James, in case she had to run from him again. When she died, I packed them away and put them in the attic. I'll go get them when I have a chance to get up there, sweetie." With that statement Carlynn fell back into her memories again, flipping through the life of Kitty.

She reared back in the chair and took another puff, setting her cigarette down on the railing. "I gave her a pair of sandals once. I took her to a dance at the college and she wore them. They were gold. Mother French braided her hair and she borrowed one of my dresses. It was ivory, and it fit her just right. She danced all night until the last song played. I never saw her as free as she was that night, all smiles and giddiness. Like a child playing in the mud for the first time." Carlynn put her hands together in a soft, joyful clap. "She looked so beautiful, I told her to keep the sandals and the dress as a gift." Carlynn smiled at the thought of the dance, and we both indulged in the mind picture of Kitty in the dress and sandals.

I looked over at Carlynn again, noticed the dark shade she was turning, and asked her what was wrong.

"She wore those sandals everywhere," she told me. "I'd see her out walking on the road and she'd have them on. One day I drove by and she was picking up trash on the side of the two-lane highway, bottles and cans and such. She had those sandals on and when I saw her bent over with a plastic bag in her hand, something inside me snapped. I pulled over a little way up the road from her. My heart broke at the sight of her picking up trash. She shouldn't have had to do that."

Carlynn put her cigarette out in the ashtray. It took her a few minutes to continue. "She saw my car and came waving to get my attention. I barely wiped my face dry before she saw me, and I got out and gave her a hug. She told me she was collecting recyclables to get the money for a washer. James didn't allow her to work, although he didn't provide for her either. He was a drunk in the worst way. Opposites attract was all I could think of when the two of them were together. She was smart and ambitious. I think of champagne when I think of Kitty—sparkly and bubbly and intoxicating."

Carlynn closed her eyes, taking a few more breaths before going on. "She loved to read and had a garden full of the best-looking vegetables and flowers. There was so much she was capable of doing, and there she was picking up other people's trash.

Don't get me wrong. There's nothing wrong about what she was doing. It was just that here was a beautiful, smart woman. My heart just broke. She was worth more than she knew or anyone else would acknowledge." Carlynn looked out to the oak tree where the fireflies used to gather. "She wore those gold sandals everywhere. She loved them because they were pretty."

I burned with the thought of it. A woman so poorly kept that she had to pick up trash to buy a washing machine angered me. James was dead. If there was a reason I wished him alive, it would be so I could wrap my hands around his throat. He died of alcoholism and meanness. My eyes flashed heat and Carlynn caught it. Looking at me, she coolly moved her head up and down in agreement with my disgust and anger.

"Well, sweetheart, maybe we should go into town now before it gets too late to be industrious." I did my best to shake off the felonious thoughts filling my head, and we spent the rest of the day running errands and visiting the locals in town.

The next morning, I slept in longer than usual. Birds were singing and the sun shone brightly through the bedroom window. Stretching lazily, and just like the day before, I rolled over to the edge of the bed and got up, still in my pajamas, wrapped myself in the quilt, and headed in the direction of the porch. Almost to the front door I spotted a note on the dining room table and went over to check it out. I recognized Carlynn's writing. She had gone into town for the sausage-gravy biscuits we both loved so much. Moving to the kitchen and pouring myself a cup of tea, I was ready to make my way to the porch once again. It was a deeply embedded part of my morning ritual.

Opening the front door and stepping through, my eyes fixed instantly on a medium-sized cardboard box sitting in front of the love seat. Covered in cobwebs and dust, it gave off a nostalgic feel. Rommel was sitting there next to it, on guard since Carlynn was in town. He whined as I pushed him off the porch. He smelled too much like dirt. Without thinking or hesitating, I sat down, relinquished the beloved cup of tea to the floor, and pulled the top off the box, pushing my hands into the heart of it and unconsciously indexing the contents. Different textures and weights of fabric filled my senses and sparked an overwhelming curiosity.

There were clothes in the box. An assortment of blouses, skirts, jeans, and dresses that looked like they would fit me. Blues, greens, reds, and pinks in a hodgepodge of hues and stages of deterioration. Exploring and happy, I picked out individual pieces, feeling them, holding them against me, and picturing Kitty in them. It was still hard to see her.

The ivory dress Carlynn had given Kitty caught my attention, and I pulled it out of the box as if starved for a closer look. When the silky material gave way, I saw something glittery sparkling at the bottom of the box. Underneath the dress sat the sandals. Gold and shiny after over a decade in the attic, they were still gorgeous. It was easy to understand why Kitty had loved them. The heel was two and a half inches high and made the back of the shoe slope at an angle to flatter even the most shapeless legs. Straps on the sides would slink up to encircle the ankles, accentuating the curve between the ball of the foot and heel. The sandals were worn on the bottom but not enough to render them useless. I sat there and looked at them for the better part of an hour and thought of how they must have made her feel.

Finally, I dared to put them on, sliding my feet into the soles. I sucked my breath in as skin connected with the faux material of the sandals. Going back and forth across the porch at least fifty times, I turned and dipped and danced until my body, heart, and feet were swept up in a sea of joy. I found myself laughing and crying at the same time, for the same reasons. They fit me perfectly. Nothing could ever be as it was before; there was no going back to ignorance.

The sound of Rommel's barking caught me off guard as he harassed Carlynn's car as it barreled up the gravel road. My eyes snapped to attention. Carlynn was home, and I didn't know whether or not I should put everything back into the box before she saw the unraveling. I hoped she had meant for me to find it. Instead of doing anything to hide my actions, I just stood on that porch like I was glued to it while the car got closer.

She got out and came up to me. I still couldn't move. She gazed past me and gave the porch a once-over, grinning like a mother when she catches her child playing in the mud in their Sunday best. She looked at my face and said nothing. Suddenly her arms were around me, and I was buried in her embrace. "I'm glad to see you found the box, honey. I wanted you to have these so it would be easier for you to see her. I knew the sandals would fit you." Emotions kept me silent as she held me in her arms.

After a few minutes, I pulled away and turned and dipped for Carlynn to see me in the sandals. I was Dorothy in her ruby slippers. Those sandals could take me anywhere I wanted to go, and that day on the porch, they were my bright and shiny passport to the past. Now I understood the sandals and Kitty, and all at once, I knew her as never before, reaching across the lost years between us. She was beautiful right down to her soul, and in those sandals she felt shiny, worthy.

Carlynn and I sat and ate the biscuits out on the porch and spent the rest of the day in town. When we got back to the house, it was beginning to get dark and dinner was late. I found Carlynn at the stove soon after we returned. Watching her prowess at frying chicken made me think of the times Kitty must have sat there watching her cook and enjoying the company.

All at once I felt guilty. "Can I help you with anything? I feel like a spoiled brat sitting here doing nothing."

With her face to the stove, she answered. "No, you just sit right there and be still. Let me spoil you a bit."

I listened and did nothing except bask in the smells of fried chicken, biscuits, and greens, just like I was told to do. I thought of the stories about Kitty and noticed the sun was all but gone. I wanted to hear more. Was ready to hear more.

"Carlynn?"

"Yes, honey?"

"Let's watch the fireflies tonight."

Carlynn turned away from the stove, half laughing.

"Yes, you have a lot of fireflies to watch."

Pausing and thinking for a minute, she reached over the sink to wash her floured hands and turned back to me again, this time in a serious tone. "And I have a lot of stories to tell."

TWELVE

Sweet Tea and Fireflies on Blalock Mountain

EVERYONE SHOULD HAVE A PORCH to sit on and linger for a while, to clear their mind and contemplate life and what means the most. And a front porch is a very good thing to have, especially if you're sitting with Carlynn Jane Manning and holding a cup of tea. On yet another Tennessee morning in Turtletown, I sat at the base of Blalock Mountain with memories of Kitty filling the air as Carlynn told me more about who she was.

Her words opened the past like an old book with notations in the white space and dog-eared corners, indicating the high points or most important parts of each story. Carlynn spoke of apple pies she and Kitty made together in her kitchen, sometimes making five and six at a time, and how the heavy, sweet smell wafting through the house would be too much for Carlynn's husband, John, to take, and he'd risk eating a few slices knowing the havoc it wrought on his diabetes. Carlynn smiled as she recalled the evenings on the porch watching the fireflies skimming the grass and softly touching the trees. Those memories making it easy to transition into more of Kitty's story and the history of what made her the battered and broken woman Carlynn knew. She called those memories Kitty's wildflower song.

KITTY

The courthouse steps felt hard beneath her. The gray stone contrasted with the brightness of the sky and made her think of the difference between what she wanted and what she had. Shielding her eyes from the early morning sun, Kitty looked once more for the red Ford pickup that held the man she loved. Remembering where she was, her downcast eyes moved from side to side as she glanced at the few passersby to see if she would be noticed. Seated firmly at the far end of the steps, she hoped to avoid scrutiny.

Kitty had snuck out of her grandmother's house that morning before the sun had come up with a paper bag full of the few clothes and the few keepsakes she had to call her own. No one knew she was gone or would even miss her until Mother needed help around the house with the eight other children. No one knew Kitty was pregnant either.

She rubbed the flat of her hand against her warm belly as subtly as she could out in the open, lingering on the slight bulge of three months of the growing baby. Then she rubbed her eyes as the heat of the sun beat down on her face, blocking her view of the road. The farthest point she could see was at the top of the hill where cars and trucks were marked by plumes of dust on that dry June day.

He said he would be there that morning. He said he loved her and wanted to marry her. The thought of Charlie filled her senses and heart. He was tall, handsome, and gentle as no man had ever been with her before, and she could picture the way he looked at her as she sat alone, waiting.

Her cousin Gerald had introduced them, and it wasn't long before they were sneaking moments together, away from the scrutiny of chastity and morals. Kitty thought Charlie was too good to be true and threw herself into every piece of his life that he would give her. He thought she was older and by the time he found out her true age, it was too late to turn back from his lover or the child they had created. She was not yet fifteen, and he had six years on her.

Charlie lay there too much in pain to focus on one exact moment. He would flash from one thought to another before the first was finished in his struggle to concentrate. But he kept going back to one thing: Kitty. She was something to look at. Rounded curves that clung to pure fire walked directly toward him that first day and smiled as a child with a secret garden to play in. It would have been easier to curse Gerald for telling him about her, but he forgot about the risk shortly after taking her in his arms. Kitty felt good and molded to his body. And she could smile. Her smile drove men wild. Men wanted what they saw, and in the mountainous North Georgia territory, some took more than they were given.

Pain jolted his senses and made him open his eyes. Or maybe they had been open before, and it was just now that he could see in a brief moment of lucidity. The sun was bright, and the blue sky was interrupted by white clouds as they moved across it. He raised his hand to his face and glimpsed the deep red of blood before dropping it to the grass again. She would be waiting for him by now and wondering where he was. Those lowlifes wanted her, he had known it from the start. He just didn't know they'd be willing to kill for her. If they only knew she was pregnant they would kindly lay down their perceived claim.

More than once Charlie had been forced to brush aside hopeful suitors to make it known that Kitty was with him and no one else. She wanted nothing to do with the others, and yet that morning two men sat waiting for Charlie's red truck to approach the bend at the abandoned farm on the outskirts of town.

Out in the solitary patch where he and Kitty frequently rendezvoused, her favorite yellow and orange wildflowers could be found. Knowing nothing of any plans for the lovers to meet at the courthouse, the men only knew that Charlie regularly kept an eye on that patch of wildflowers and would eventually wind up there to cut a bouquet or wait for Kitty to arrive. More than once, the men watched the young couple in the field, playing at being a couple and making love. Today, they found an opportunity to reduce the threat of Kitty vanishing from their fantasy world.

Charlie was caught with his back to them, crouched over the yellow and orange, choosing what would befit a bride on her wedding day. He got lost in the heady fragrance of past visits as he picked the flowers. Kitty and Charlie had spent days in the array of dazzling color, soaking in the sun and dreaming together. Before he could tear loose from the thoughts of his past with Kitty, fisted hands drew knives and hovered just above his waist. Preying on his surprise, they attacked him with a furious momentum, leaving little hope of life. The blades pushed in and ripped flesh as he fell to the ground, descending into heat and blinding pain.

Left alone and helpless, he felt the blades of grass and wildflowers flopping against his skin in the slight breeze, reminding him to breathe. The stab wounds pulsed, and he closed his eyes, dreaming of softness and light as his blood seeped into the ground. He ached from the attack and the thought of Kitty without him. He could hear her voice telling him that she loved him and to come and be with her.

———————————

Kitty fumbled with her shoes. The same shoes that the nice lady at church gave to her when her own had been walked in a year too long. She moved her fingers across the patent leather, vainly trying to shine them with spit. They were like most of her clothes, worn and faded. She didn't care. There were more important things for her to worry about now than the purchase of a new dress or pretty shoes. Soon there would be a husband and a baby. Charlie would come, she just knew it, although it was getting late.

Mrs. Parker from next door had seen Kitty sitting on the courthouse steps and told her grandmother, even if that information didn't matter to most. Mrs. Parker could be counted on to tattle. Kitty had been the source of gossip many times in the past and was getting used to the dirty looks and the stares women gave her. Men liked her and she liked the attention and privilege being pretty afforded her. It was the only power she owned.

She had already gotten pregnant just a year and a half before and had to give the baby away to a woman who had a husband. The first baby was a boy, and Kitty had tried to keep him but wasn't able to because she was on her own for the most part. One more mouth to feed was too much for the family. Everybody knew about the baby boy and blamed Kitty for the mistake of wanting to be touched. The baby wasn't important to anyone but her.

She wouldn't let them take away this baby. It was hers and Charlie's. She would wait all day if she had to, no matter who saw her, no matter what anyone thought of her. Charlie was her only hope, her redeemer, and she would wait for him.

———————————

The youngest of the three boys came up on the farm field first, and you would have thought he had found gold. There's nothing like the sight of a bloody man to set the imagination of a ten-year-old reeling into some faraway place of adventure and excitement. He stopped short and repented when he thought it over. His brothers moved fast, crouching over the body and checking for life, better understanding the intensity of this moment. Charlie opened his eyes as the two older boys hoisted his limp frame between theirs and slowly made a path in the grass to get some help. He touched the yellow and orange flowers for the last time as his feet dragged. He spent weeks in the hospital recovering from stab wounds and the loss of so much blood. As soon as he was released, he escaped to Florida. There had been threats of another attack. By the time he got back to check on Kitty, the baby was gone, and she was a different woman.

The sun was setting, and the courthouse was closed for the day. The last of the custodians pitifully asked her if she was all right. They had seen her from the morning on and only guessed at her intent on staying there so long. She was hungry and thirsty, but that was the best part of this day. She looked through the kind face and lied, telling the custodian she was fine and just waiting for a ride. When everyone had left the courthouse, Kitty sat alone and hung her head in shame and desperation at the thought of losing another baby. The sun finally went down, and hours after she first set out to wait for hope, she stood up to return to the loneliness she would grow accustomed to.

Carlynn finished Kitty's story and then asked me if I had met any of the birth mothers. I told her I had talked to a handful and heard their stories, but because of all the chaos before and after the story broke in 1997 and my attention turning toward my career, I hadn't spent as much time with them as I wanted. She nodded her head and looked out to the yard. We sat for a while, and then Carlynn began to tell me the story of Twyla, a good friend of hers, who had gotten caught up in the Hicks Clinic some years before.

TWYLA

She sat in the darkness of the shed for hours, shaking from fear and pain and waiting for him to come back and rape her again. The holes in the wooden wall gave her an idea of what time it was, whether it was day or night. Her cracked lips burned, and her tongue was too swollen and dry to soothe them. The kids would wonder where she was and why she wasn't home yet. "The kids," she muttered to herself. "They'll never understand why their daddy would do this."

She leaned her head against the splintered walls of the shed and tried to relax. Thoughts of what she could do to get out and run pushed rest from her mind even though her body sorely needed it. With a jolt, the reality of the moment came to her. "Jesus! He's not going to come and let me out. He's going to kill me! Oh God, no! Please help me." With that she was reeling against the pain and exhaustion again. She had to get out.

Groping for something to hold on to, she knocked over a pile of large metal cans and an old ladder, all of which fell to the ground in a loud roar. Her hands flew up to her ears, the instinctive move mocked her intentions of being quiet. Shaking, Twyla began praying under her breath like an innocent child reciting the Lord's Prayer. She tried again to stand on her bruised and bloodied legs. "God, please don't let him hear me.

Please let me get out of here. Please let me get home to my babies."

Dogs barked in the distance and fear took hold as she heard the familiar purr of her husband's truck and the crunching of gravel under its tires. In advanced surrender, she slid down the wall to the dirt floor, leaving more gouges in her back as the splinters dug through her shredded dress. But she felt nothing. There were no more tears left to cry. She had little choice in what he would do to her. She couldn't keep fighting. Maybe he would be merciful and let her live.

The door flung open and Twyla's wild-eyed husband screamed his drunken arrival once again. She raised her hands over her head in an attempt to protect herself. The scent of gin, or something close to it, permeated the air as he spewed his venom at her. Fear and the smell of him made Twyla gulp, fighting back the bile rising in her throat.

"You worthless dog. Look at you. You can't even stand up. You are a mess." He grabbed her hair and pulled straight up until her feet were flat on the ground.

This was the third day she had spent in the shed, and he was on his fourth day of drinking. Twyla had been naive to think he was being helpful when he pulled up alongside her outside the Piggly Wiggly. She had only wanted a ride home, and it had been just a few days since he'd called to say he was sorry about the drinking and wanted to come home.

Now he stood before her as master, eyes glazed over and boring holes into her. Holding her by her hair and glaring hate, he showed her all that she had feared in a man. She tried hard to focus on his face so he wouldn't stop talking, hoping he had only come back for a verbal attack. But she knew better. The dogs were still baying outside, and the sound haunted her as the distraction bore its way into her mind. Her head spun and the light faded as the weight of him pushed against her swollen body. Once again, she lost ground and any thread of dignity she could find as she lay filthy and beaten on the dirt floor of the shed.

Light streamed in from above, shining across her face as she came to. The sound of the children's voices permeated the walls like ghosts and then faded with each moment as it became clearer that she had not found her way out of the shed. Another morning and more pain. Her head was beating out a rhythm with the aches in the rest of her body. It was morning, wasn't it? She must have been unconscious all night. When her head stopped pulsing, she dared to look at her legs and feet. They didn't look familiar. Her arms ached and were wrung with bruises like snakes wrapping and encircling her swollen skin. She sat looking at the filth that covered her and almost cared.

The quilt was soft and smelled of fresh lemon. Flowers on the bedside table moved slightly with the breeze coming in the window. Through the same window, she could see all three of her children as they played in the yard. She cried every now and again when she saw her babies because she hadn't thought she would see them again. She could hear familiar voices in the next room. She was staying with a friend named Caroline and was grateful to her for taking such good care in nursing her back to health.

Twyla prayed her thanks to God and lay there watching the children.

And she felt clean.

Twyla didn't know what to say to a man so polished and professional. Doc Hicks sat across from her at his desk and asked her questions she hadn't thought of before and would later try to forget.

"Whatcha going to do with the baby, Twyla? Do you have enough money to feed it? Or how about paying my fee for delivering it?"

She could only nod. She had no money. And now she had no husband to help with the bills another baby would bring. She put her head down and shook it.

Doc Hicks rubbed his chin and pushed his feet hard against the floor until his chair started to tip backward. He gave her a once-over. "I've heard you're a good cook."

"Yes, I guess so. I worked at the restaurant."

"You can cook and clean for my wife to work off the expense of taking care of your pregnancy, whether you abort it or have it. But I advise you to let me find the baby a good home, especially seeing that you don't have a husband no more. And brand-new babies are easier to find a home for." Hicks clicked his tongue. "You sure he's not coming back? I don't want any complications if he does come back, ya know? Since I am helping you out and all."

"Yes, sir. I mean, he's not coming back." Twyla's mind raced at the thought of giving her baby to strangers, to anyone. She rubbed her stomach. This was her baby. Tears began again as she failed to fight them back.

Doc Hicks saw her groping for an answer. "You could abort it. How far along are you? You said it was a rape? Hmm. It's up to you. Let me know. The sooner the better."

Twyla walked out the door of the Hicks Clinic and sat down on the front stoop. Her kids were with Caroline and she had to be at work soon. She was too tired and alone to make this decision. She sat there and wrestled with the facts at hand. Three kids. One job that barely made ends meet. Handouts from the church. No husband. No relatives who could help her out for any period of time. She went through the list twice and stepped back into the clinic. She had no choice.

She asked the nurse if she could see the doctor and proceeded to walk back to his office. She hardened herself for what she must do. That day the walls of the shed began to rebuild themselves in Twyla's heart, reminding her that she was doing the best thing for the baby.

"Doc Hicks, did you say you could find a good home for my baby?"

The doctor smiled and started talking about nice couples from Ohio and how he was looking forward to eating her cooking. He had heard such good things about her cooking.

When Carlynn finished Twyla's story, she must have seen the look on my face. She smiled and told me to get my shoes on because she had someone she wanted me to meet. We drove through Turtletown and picked up a burger and a Coke at Hardees, then proceeded through Ducktown and on into Mc-Caysville and even a bit farther until we stopped at a tiny house set a-ways off the road. Carlynn parked the car at the bottom of a steep path that led to the front door of the house. With a smile and a light, almost excited tone, she asked, "Would you like to meet Twyla? She wants to meet you."

And that's how Carlynn would introduce me to birth mothers. She took me to meet them so I would know them, not just hear of their lives. She made me take a good long look at each and love them as she had. She wanted me to see the struggle and longing these women had endured in their lives and understand why or how they lost their babies. They wanted healing, understanding, and sometimes just someone to listen to their story. Those women and their stories opened a door into a room I hadn't dared enter when I was searching for clues, facts, or records. They were firsthand accounts of how a life could be interrupted by, well, by life.

It was always an adventure with Carlynn, but her adventures always meant something more. They were embedded with the truth of what love is. A truth that you don't want to wait to the end of your life to find. It was as though God's love for these women and Carlynn's as well was redeeming the time lost for me and restoring the lonely years of my search.

Years of visiting with birth mothers, sitting and sharing a cup of tea or a Coke, meant so much to me and to other Hicks Babies who would join Carlynn and me. They might have thought they were in town looking to spend time on Carlynn's porch but would find themselves whisked off to meet a birth mother. A lot of these women knew each other through a myriad of circumstances. Carlynn knew what meant the most to the birth mothers and the babies and did what she could to merge the two.

It was 2005. It was cold outside, and I was back at the Manning household in Tennessee for the holiday. The fireplace was roaring and toasty. Christmas was a couple days away, so Carlynn and I sat in the kitchen instead of on the porch. We warmed our hands with our signature cups of tea for our usual chatting, dinner planning, and plotting of any adventures we could muster up. Out of the blue, Carlynn started talking about Kitty and the way she used to take long walks up the mountain. She told me how much Kitty loved to be out and about, even in the cold. She had told Carlynn how it cleared her mind. It was rumored Kitty had a friend that she'd meet up there to picnic with and find some sense of belonging.

We chatted back and forth about how we wished for some way to find the boy Kitty had given up a year or so before me.

Carlynn's voice took on the soft, serious tone that always brought me to attention. "I want you to promise me something."

I agreed without even thinking about it. "Of course."

"If for some reason, now, I can't fathom it, but if we ever find out Kitty wasn't your mother"—she stopped and stared into my eyes until she was sure I was 100 percent listening—"if she's not yours, I want you to promise you'll find her babies and tell them how much she loved them. Tell them how beautiful she was inside and out."

We both knew there was the possibility I wasn't Kitty's daughter but never really considered it since I was so much like her and so many pieces fit. Carlynn got up and gave me a hug, and I told her I would.

We found our way back to the porch in the spring. We spent so many evenings laughing and crying on that porch, they all blur together. Thousands of pieces and bits of my memory are strewn across the wooden floorboards of the porch like metallic gold and silver confetti to sift through. John would join us and pepper our talks with a joke or some light gossip he'd heard from the golf club. I once asked him if I could get a lesson or two with the golf pro at the club one time and he told me, "Janie, if you go over to the club, those golf pros will be happy to give you a lesson. Why, they'll start you out with the irons and do everything in their skill level to finish up with you in the woods." But then he shook his head and laughed, saying there was no way he would allow those men near me. Carlynn and I busted out in fits of laughter and he grinned and flashed his baby blues in satisfaction as he watched us having a good time. Some days he'd poke his head out the front door and ask us what we were doing. When we told him we were talking about what had happened in town that day or even the week before, he'd tsk-tsk us and say it sounded like gossiping and retreat back into the house only to grab his cigarettes and his coffee to join us again a minute or two later, asking us to start the conversation from the beginning again so he could catch up. And there we would sit like three amigos.

Carlynn passed in the spring of 2009, three years after John. I loved them both with my everything and it took years to overcome their leaving me behind. Although I had them for just over a decade, it seemed like I had just found them. It was almost unbearable when Carlynn was gone, but I had a promise to keep. It took some time to have the heart to look for my brother without her. But I tucked away as much of the silver and gold confetti in my heart as I could and set out to find Kitty's baby boy.

THIRTEEN

The Rise and Fall

AUTHOR LOUISA MAY ALCOTT WROTE, "I like adventures and I'm going to find some."* Me too, but sometimes they find me before I have a chance to seek them out. And then, well, it gets a little crazy and out of hand. I'm always up for an adventure, but one day in 2015, I sat looking at the DNA kit from Ancestry.com like it was a foreign object, not enthusiastic about what was to be done. Although I was aware that DNA technology had advanced incredibly since 1997 when we had done the first tests, I'd avoided going with a big-box DNA company in order to remain as private as possible.

Fellow Hicks Baby Mark Eckenrode had told me of his experience, and I decided to use the same site. It was the best one due to its number of members if I wanted to find my brother, Kitty's boy. The phone rang, busting me out of my thoughts. It was Michelle.

---

* Louisa May Alcott, *Little Women* (Boston: Roberts Brothers, 1868), 71.

"Janie, I need your help with this. I don't know what to do now." She had decided to do another DNA test as many in the group had.

I smiled at the perfect timing of Michelle's call to accentuate the need for me to get my test completed and sent off. I completed my kit and off it went to Ancestry that same day.

Michelle continued, "I've got a match with a high number and don't know what I want to do. This is crazy!" She was serious one moment and chuckling the next. Her energy was contagious.

We cracked our usual jokes about being from the Hicks Clinic and then discussed the next steps, how to connect the dots and then how to connect. Wherever her journey was taking her, she was finally ready. Years after the first DNA test in 1997, she wanted to find out more about her birth story. She had been battling cancer for several years and wanted to find medical information for her three boys. She was in her last days. Her cancer had come back with a vengeance, and we worked her DNA family tree as quickly as possible, piecing it together while I waited for my results. Her high-numbered DNA connection ended up being a birth mother, and we decided to proceed with caution.

Six weeks later, I sat looking at the computer screen, incredulous at the results of my own test. I opened my Ancestry account and began looking at the matches. "Oh, God, help me." No matter how many times I searched the list, the person I expected to see wasn't there. Like a rush of wind, I prayed those words again, this time with a hint of desperation and unbelief. I had DNA matches, but none had a connection to Kitty. Nothing to bring our two gene pools together. Suddenly, my entire sense of family history stopped.

Centimorgans, those little DNA markers of fact checking, are a unit of genetic measurement. They're what experts use to describe how much DNA you share with your relatives and the length of specific segments of DNA. The more centimorgans you share with someone, the closer you're related. Although I was cursing the little markers and shaking my head at their unwelcome entry into my world, they are the basis of every DNA test and provide the connectors, like the wiring and spark plugs of who you are. No one can deny the trail they create or the confirmation they give. Centimorgans can turn everything you thought to be true on its head. The truth of my DNA results had not just provided a hiccup in what I thought was my life story, it had wiped clean the only family tree I knew. Right down to the roots.

I had stopped my search for family because I thought I found it, and once Carlynn had passed, I placed myself on standby, just filtering Hicks Clinic leads for some noteworthy spark and picking and choosing how and who I would help with their search. And then this. How was I going to tell Tabitha and Charlie? For seventeen years I thought they were my sister and my father. Charlie was the man Kitty had loved and said he was the father of her baby girl, and Tabitha was his daughter from his marriage. They were my story, my family, as much as Kitty had been, and I accepted that binding with them. That part of my tapestry was set in place. I was stunned into silence and numbness. I sat staring at the screen for some time, breaking down a little bit with each moment until there were tears on my cheeks.

I reached up to wipe them away, and it was then that I remembered and heard Carlynn's soft, reassuring voice gently commanding me, clear as I had heard it many times before while sitting at her feet as tears flowed from life's challenges. Her voice flooded me. "Now dry your eyes, honey, you've cried enough. It's time to dry them and move on to do what you have to do. You can do this. You can." Gasping for breath and trying to pull in my emotions, the tears finally stopped, and I dried my eyes long enough to look at the DNA matches in front of me. It was time to get started with the search once again.

Like soldiers in formation, my DNA info lined up in two distinct rows. The big question was which side was which and how and where I should start. Paternal or maternal? Before I could begin messaging all of the willing participants on my genetic tree to ask who they were and if they knew how I fit in, a young woman named Jeannie reached out to me. She said she was my second cousin. She seemed to have a good grasp on Ancestry and how to navigate it. She was pretty sure she was from my father's side, because we shared that genetic line. And then she began to flesh out the basics of my maternal side and the variations that could pop up. She told me I was from the Hunnicut family line from the Carolinas and North Georgia area around Blue Ridge who had settled in the area. When I finally pulled myself away from pondering and dreaming, I began calling my matches, starting with the first cousins.

On the first call I struck gold, like Beverly Hillbillies gold. It came out of nowhere, but it was really, really good and changed everything. My newfound cousin Amy listened to me, and I could tell she was stymied, but she was patient and took down my information. After we chatted and hung up, it didn't take long before she was calling me back after asking her father a few questions. She had had no idea about me or an adoption, but she filled me in on details about a baby who was very likely me. Confirmed through DNA with her and several other family members, I now knew my maternal side of the tree. Amy told me the story of Bonnie Mae, the woman who turned out to be my grandmother, and I sat listening in awe as she shared the milestones of this matriarch's life. Some of those milestones elicited some giggling and some full-out belly laughs as her life was painted with words in bright colors and broad brushstrokes on a stark white canvas.

My twin uncles, William and Wesley, heard about me from Cousin Amy when she called her father and told him how I was searching, how I had been born at the Hicks Clinic. I met my uncles, and we spent time getting acquainted. They introduced me to other family members: my great-aunt Betty, uncle Harve, cousins Joe and Opal Brawley—some of my favorites. They told me of life growing up with Bonnie Mae and the generations of Hunnicuts before her. I loved every minute listening to the details of their lives and how Bonnie had been as a mother. I tried to keep on an even keel and fought to stay controlled until I heard stories of her bootlegging moonshine and keeping a fair number of the locals stocked with some of the best homemade liquor that could be found. The belly laughs took over and I almost fell out of my chair. My grandmother was a bootlegging businesswoman. That was not too surprising to me because of my own quirky, wild side, and then I laughed more and more as the stories kept coming.

They told more stories than I can recount about Bonnie and my grandfather, Bunyan, the seven-foot-tall farmer who lived to care for his animals and land. Hardworking and content with life, save a few rough moments of bickering while at odds with each other, which led to some eyebrow-raising events. Bonnie and Bunyan lived into their late sixties. Bonnie's family had come from England to America. William and Wesley told stories of my great-grandfather's and great-great-grandfather's careers as preachers and how they had heard my great-grandfather, Joseph Hunnicut, preaching on the radio in Copperhill. I was intrigued. If I could locate recordings of Joseph Hunnicut, that would be the closest way I could experience hearing the voice of any of the previous generations of my ancestors who had passed. So, I went looking for the recordings at the radio station in Copperhill, but they couldn't be found.

After several calls and pleas to local contacts and anyone with connections to the recordings, I sat in the overstuffed chair in my living room, frustrated and making little girl faces reminiscent of a tantrum because I couldn't hear Joseph's preaching. I longed to hear the voice that I imagined was low and direct, a voice that would settle me. I pushed deeper into the comfy cushions on the chair with my back and legs like a tantrum-prone child trying to make my will speak louder than anyone else or anything. After a few moments of haughtiness, it hit me that through all the years of my growing up and feeling like I had been protected through the hard times, it became clear someone had been praying for me even though they didn't know me. I was a part of the future generations as they prayed over their familial lines like Abraham and David. They knew their prayers would not come back void. Imagining Joseph's voice, beautiful words of obedience and faithfulness sang through my mind like the redemptive love songs of Ruth and Esther. My great-grandfather had preached to the good people of North Georgia and across the state line of Tennessee and his words and his preaching still stood true. The circle of life sometimes circles back to pick up some of its pieces, my pieces.

The next time I spoke on the phone with my uncle William, I told him I couldn't get my hands on the tapes. He made me feel better as he told me more about Grandpa Joe and how when he was around ten to twelve years old, he had gone to the radio station while his grandpa preached. Joe Hunnicut, standing in front of the big silver microphone and talking with the fire of a Baptist preacher, his voice going up in range as much as in volume. That would've been around 1969. My uncle's exuberance for our grandfather's contribution to Georgia's spiritual life was clear, and I now shared it with him. Smiling bigger than ever, I conveyed my thoughts and excitement and planned our next meeting, discussing how we would revisit the good restaurant that makes my favorite chicken livers.

"Wesley and I have more stories and we can all meet up at the restaurant. We got plenty of good times and getting-in-trouble stories!" He laughed as I pulled out my calendar to note the best days to travel to Georgia. I was looking forward to time with my uncles and cousins Joe and Opal and everyone else in the family line. Like so many times before, I packed a bag and threw it into the car and headed south, trying to get there before the sun went down.

On cue, I made it just before sundown. Sounds of the mountain swirled around me as I sat on the back deck of the Brawley house, the North Georgia breeze mingling among the colossal-sized wind chimes touching each other in a melody. Cousin Joe had said to stop by and see the chimes that ranged from two feet to as big as eight feet tall, as well as the family cemetery out back. The Brawleys were connected to the Hunnicuts and had lived close to one another for decades. Now that I was a part of the family, I might be interested to see it, he thought. And I was. The sun was going down, and the crickets added a crescendo a few times throughout the windsong coming together around me. I could see Joe's brother's grave marker from the back deck in the cemetery up on the hill behind the house. The marker was tall and made of stone and was by all accounts a work of art.

Joe and Opal opened their home and lives to me and told me I had a right to know who I was and who my family was too. My thankfulness at the nod to my feelings and rights was too overwhelming to express. I looked around their yard as my mind wandered and thought of the peacefulness of this place, the belonging and the heritage I'd missed for all those years, both good times and bad. Would I have played in the grass just over across from the driveway or in the fields just off the road? I thought of Michelle. She had passed less than a year before she could meet her birth mother. Though she hadn't gotten the chance to meet her, Michelle did find a sister and learn of her maternal side before losing her battle. I didn't tell her I had found anything; I didn't want her to think she would be replaced when she was gone. She would've liked this place and the chimes. The invitation to visit here was a gift to me, and I listened as the breeze lilted through the chimes, as though it had a slightly upturned chin, gently challenging them to sing to me, to sing a new song. As the sun disappeared and the chimes kept on, the challenge was fulfilled with a serenade that stretched across those fields, rolling for some distance.

After a good night's rest, I met up with my uncles and we started yapping and laughing all over again. My favorite memories they shared were stories of their youth—running all around the area, fishing and hunting, and sketchy times they spent being around when Bonnie was bootlegging out the back of her store, located on the bend in the road, not too far from where the Brawley house stands today. They mentioned with a wink that she may or may not have done a little time for bootlegging. I made a notation to check on that further when I had a chance. William and Wesley threw out some more winks of their own shenanigans and a story about poaching deer at night, knowing full well it was illegal. They described how it was dark out and how it was challenging to stay quiet for two young boys in an old beat-up pickup truck, try as they might. They were just kids then, having fun and playing games. After two years of chasing the boys for poaching, the game warden caught up to them one night out of nowhere, and without skipping a beat, took them both by the collar and asked what they were doing, respectfully rubbing in the victory of finally catching them. They mentioned his name. Herbert Cruce.

FOURTEEN

A Beautiful Dance

H E WAS THE SON of a good man. Tommy was a child of the sixties and grew into the seventies, and I couldn't have been more pleased to hear his voice on the other end of the phone. My newly found cousin Donna was a DNA match, and she quickly directed me to her cousin Tommy because she had a hunch I was his sister. Picture a man with a long, wild beard, boots, and worn Levi's, the Eagles song "Take It Easy" playing in your head, Arizona sun, flatbed Ford, and all. At eighteen he took off from Georgia on his motorcycle. After a childhood marred by his parents' divorce, something he couldn't overcome in his rebellious teens, Tommy was looking for a life of adventure in the West and seeking a soft place to lay his head. Now sixty-six, twelve years older than me, we were on the phone and I was hearing the voice of my newly found brother for the first time.

Long years with drugs, time spent going from woman to woman, and a general sense of abandonment had pushed his life forward. He had gone through some rough times over the years. But he was quick to take accountability for his actions. He stepped up and made sure I knew he blamed no one for the mistakes he had made. Tommy said his father had taught him right. They were his choices and he owned them. He had finally found a good landing place. He'd been stable for twenty years, he'd found the love of a good woman and friends to credit, and he had made his way to peace.

His voice was gravelly but with a tone that was genuine and fun. We talked and compared notes of our lives. We both had a wild and rebellious side and offered each other listening ears, playing compare and contrast for a couple of hours. We had traded pictures earlier that week, so we knew we had the same nose, but our conversation taught us about our mutual love for music that spans genres. We had both grown up with the freedom to make our own choices; we were left to ourselves mostly. Giving each other a rundown of our lives felt good. I immersed myself in the fact that I had a brother. A cool, fun one at that.

That call took place in February 2018, and Tommy passed in the middle of the night in December 2019. I lost him as fast as I found him. A thousand times I've said that God knows what He's doing, and I have to embrace what happens no matter how hard and disappointing. He saw Tommy, He saw me from the beginning, and He saw Tommy's baby girl too. A call from Tommy's wife soon after he passed filled in the details about Tommy's daughter, Alyssa, born in February 1996. Tommy's wife told me he barely saw Alyssa before she was adopted, and he hadn't seen her since. After Tommy passed, she contacted Alyssa and they reconnected. Then she added that Alyssa and I looked a lot alike. That made me smile. She told me as much as she knew: that

Alyssa had been adopted by a wonderful family that protected and raised her to be a strong and talented young woman.

Curiosity in full tilt, I looked this unknown niece up, and I was soon scrolling through her life in a montage of pictures and time lines and milestone events documented on social media. I clicked on a video of her that deadstopped me in awe. As I watched a live performance, Alyssa's voice filled the air around me. It was beautiful. As she played the guitar, with eyes closed and her long brown hair flowing around her face, her words called out to attest to the love of God.

> Even on my worst days You call me beautiful one
> Words are not enough for Him, so by His hands I'm
>   made
> Stitched together with His love
> So, I'll sing His name
> Mighty Warrior, King, Abba Father, Hosanna
> You are worthy of praise
> Jesus Savior, You are my Redeemer, my shelter
> When I need out of the rain.

Her voice had Tommy's deep, colorful tone, and if it is possible to hear the earth's raw richness singing, it would be through her words exploding with strong, soulful insights. And she looked like me. I was surprised to see her look so much like me. She was a twenty-three-year-old, hipper-than-I've-ever-been version of me. She had never met Tommy, like I had never met my birth father, her grandfather.

Tommy's DNA confirmed that I was Herbert Claud Cruce's daughter. My Ancestry tree had several first cousin matches that pointed me in the right direction, but Tommy was the firstborn on my father's side and our DNA matched. My cousin Donna proved to be a strong, wonderful woman who offered her help freely and welcomed me to the family, even before we knew exactly where I fit in. Donna listened to my story several times and began sharing pictures of Herbert and my paternal grandparents, Maude Estelle and Claud. To my delight, Donna pointed out how much I looked like Grandma Cruce, and I pored over all the pictures and listened to every story. A little over a year later, I found myself at the Cruce family reunion, listening to Cousin Phil give the history of the seven boys and three girls Grandma and Grandpa Cruce raised with love and hard work.

Grandma Cruce's daddy was a preacher and pastored the Yellow River Baptist Church outside of Atlanta from 1912 to 1931. Her mother's name was Tallulah and she was a good cook who had eleven babies herself. I liked having someone named Tallulah in my family line. When I heard it, it just seemed right. Grandma Maude lived to be ninety-five, and she raised her children and grandchildren to respect God and each other. Not gossiping but standing shoulder to shoulder together. They were hard workers and lived through some difficult times, but they came through together as a family. I sat at the reunion, listening to the details of the years' worth of life and stories draped in laughter and others told with tears, and I found myself wishing I had had a front-row seat to the life of the Cruce family.

"Rooted in Spain and immigrating to Ireland for a couple generations and then to America, their ancestors settled in the Atlanta area. The Claud and Maude Cruce family history as we know it today goes like this: they grew up as poor cotton pickers, farming and doing pickup work before moving on to work at a service station to stay alive. They lived through the Great Depression and the war to end all wars with everyone staying intact . . ."

I heard my cousin's words as he continued to give the Cruce family story. "Herbert was in the Army Air Corps, which later became the Air Force. He was a tail gunner on the B-17 bombers flying from England to Germany."

The Great Depression, having to pick cotton to survive, and all the details Cousin Phil was filling in for the whole family rang through my mind like a smooth and soft church bell at noon. The gentle chiming pushed me to pursue more than DNA matches. I wanted to see the connections and feel the movement of the generations in my path. The Cruce family was real and alive and vibrant. Long days in cotton fields and the silky softness of the small white tufts lined my thoughts like the painted-on clouds of that baby book I had found so many years before. Sandwich routes driven from stop to stop to feed the hungry and make a living to feed the family and carve out a better life. Loving grandparents who raised ten children to be good people. I listened to every word, every intonation, and every insight and was lost in the stories. My family served in World War II–Europe, Iwo Jima, and Guam. One of the Cruce boys had even served under General Patton at the Battle of the Bulge.

When I heard Herbert's name associated with the words *Air Corps*, *B-17*, and *tail gunner*, everything else Phil said from that point was mine. My highly romanticized relationship with the World War II era, the "greatest generation of our time," and the fight between good and evil had just upped the ante for me. *This is good*, that's all I could think as I sat listening. The stories they told of Herbert made him seem larger than life, and I was smiling at the goodness of hearing his history. Tail gunners were known for their nerves of steel, ability to stay calm. Phil mentioned Herbert enjoying his way across Europe. I love looking at the faded pictures Donna gave me of my birth father in his army uniform. They make me think how handsome he was and how proud I am to be from the Cruce family, that highly sought-after heritage not taken for granted for a second. Phil kept telling stories of the Cruce boys kicking butt in World War II, and I made a mental note to follow up with him later. Herbert's journey was coming to life before my eyes, and Phil's words were soaking into my heart like a heavy rain.

When Herbert returned from the war, he made his way north of Atlanta to Suches and was appointed game warden over the area and on up to the Tennessee line by Zell Miller himself before the late politician became the governor of Georgia. Phil finished his talk on the Cruce family, and we all chatted over dinner. He and another cousin were discussing Herbert as we stood there, and they laughed, elbowing each other as they painted a picture of Herbert as freewheeling. They said he let the ladies fall in love with him, right up to his last marriage when he finally settled down with the woman he loved and had three children, many years after Tommy and me.

These cousins talked of Herbert's love of dancing starting in his teen years in the community halls around Atlanta at Clarkston, Lilburn, and Gloster. They told me how he didn't miss a night at the dance hall in Suches. Greater than his love of dancing was his love of his family and the outdoors. He was extraordinarily physically fit. At a previous reunion, at seventy-five years old, Herbert did a succession of backflips across the lawn to everyone's delight and astonishment. All the other boys in the family had lost their hair, but Herbert's seemed to get thicker, increasingly more bountiful, and downright unruly as he aged. And he liked showing it off too. There were so many cousins there all sharing what they knew. It was an afternoon to remember. They told stories of the fun and games my father loved and how everyone loved him. There wasn't enough time to hear it all, and I was one of the last to leave, not wanting to miss one moment of being included, of being a Cruce.

In the days that followed, I kept recalling the reunion details day and night. I allowed my imagination to move me to the dance hall to picture my father dancing the night away with the Georgia beauties. Smoothly skimming his heels across a scuffed wooden floor to grab the attention or the hand of a pretty, vivacious young woman. I imagined Herbert's direct smile and bright eyes as he danced and laughed. The black-and-white pictures of him weren't fading into shades of gray. It was as though color was pouring over them and filling in what was hiding in the background. What I would do to match his steps to my steps and dance with him just once and see his crazy unruly hair and that smile.

I knew the area of Suches. I'd been through it several times on my way to McCaysville. I'd sat on the porch at the Brawley house there. It's a gorgeous area and not too far from the town where I was born. Open blue sky stretches seemingly forever, and rushing streams in lush landscapes wrap around mile-high pines. The town's dotted with few roads and no strip malls to mar the view of the great outdoors. Just beauty and sunshine.

These were his stomping grounds, and he owned them with respect as the game warden. Herbert watched over his area of responsibility with diligence and care, frequently making right what had gone wrong and making it home for dinner, sometimes sharing a story or two with his sons and daughter.

On my way down to the outskirts of Atlanta to meet Alyssa, I pulled into the drive at the Brawley house to take in the town again, as though I couldn't get enough of Suches. Everything I've heard of Herbert has been a montage of the man. Pictures and stories of where and how he lived. I learned that he had a calm and careful way with people, meting out justice with fairness and flair.

His second-oldest son told me about a time when he was a teen, and he and Herbert had been out fishing. While on the drive home, Herbert had spotted a couple men breaking the rules and stopped to talk with them. He had such a way to him that delicately demanded respect and yet also got the job done. He could pull a bad guy to the right side with ease and hospitality. Herbert had those two men fill out their own citations, and he smiled as they thanked him profusely for the tickets they had just written to themselves. Delicate times demand respect and commitment to service, and he knew what that was and lived it.

One foot in the car and the other on the gravel of the drive, I looked up at the sun shining bright. Taking a deep breath and filling my lungs with the smell of pine and damp soil, I thought of moonshine and wondered if Herbert ever crossed paths with Bonnie or heard Great-grandpa Hunnicut preaching on the radio. And those chimes from the backyard, I could hear those chimes in the distance, up on the hill by the house, the sounds serenading me again. And I listened, I wanted to just be there.

Donna and many others in the Cruce family have assured me that Herbert would never have let me be taken away. He would've taken me in himself, if only he had known I existed. They were sure he didn't know. No one did. They said Grandma Cruce would've raised me. That thought consoles me, and I love them for saying it. They didn't have to; they could've let it be, but they wanted me to know. Life is life and it's beautiful in all of its imperfections and detours. They are all beautiful people, and they're mine. Life is circular and connected in ways we will never be fully aware of, and I don't want to take any of it for granted.

Looking back at the Cruce reunion, thinking of my twin uncles slapping each other's backs and laughing about how the game warden caught them after two years and could've been a tyrant with them but wasn't, and letting my mind wander through the days and nights that Herbert owned the rugged and beautiful territory of North Georgia, I can't help but see him.

Remembering the time when I was sitting with my twin uncles as they laughed and joked about their youth, of being young and carefree—or to use their phrase, "stupid for thinking Herbert Cruce wouldn't catch up to us." They buzzed in, "We knew your daddy, very well." They both nodded and became reverent, the young boys in them reined in. And though I'd heard these words many times from newfound family and strangers alike who knew Herbert and knew the kind of man he was, I heard the words with my heart as my uncles said them.

"He was a good man."

FIFTEEN

Taken at Birth—
The Opening Act

I F YOU'VE EVER seen a wasp's nest fall to the ground and explode into a hot, buzzing mess, you can understand why I was apprehensive. In 2017 TLC approached me about a docuseries on the Hicks Clinic. The last time I had worked on a project including cameras and anything connected to the clinic, my life turned upside down. But there were still birth mothers out there to be found. I set aside my worries, and TLC messaged me to say I should expect a call from the producer soon so we could go over the details and get everything started.

Chaney Moon called me, and with a calm voice, she introduced herself as the producer of the series. She shared stories of her life, wanting me to know she could be trusted and would pour her heart into getting to know the details of the Hicks Clinic and all those connected to the story. She was set on getting it right.

I asked her if she was ready for us. The story broke in 1997 but by 2017, it had grown and fermented. Chaney and I talked for over two hours, and I gave her the high-level brief of the story as I knew it and asked a good number of questions of her as well. It was a good conversation on the phone but during the time we spent face-to-face, sitting in the parlor at the Blue Ridge Inn, the big picture began to come together for her. Until then, she was an outsider on the fringe of a story, working another production. This was her expertise, and she came to Georgia to capture all of the details for the world to see. Sitting there at the inn, with its obvious step back into the past and its Southern-soaked history, her understanding went from a quiet filing of the details to a shared quest for closure. She wanted us to win.

As with all of the others who asked, the best way I could think to convey what Doc Hicks had done was to tell the stories I'd collected from those tied to the clinic. I told Chaney about the birth mothers I'd known over the years and how they each had a pain and longing in their hearts, no matter their circumstances. They were still hurting, they felt guilt, and they wanted to be understood. I told stories of Carlynn and our adventures together, my sources, and the town of Mc-Caysville. I shared my love for the good food at my favorite Copperhill and McCaysville restaurants, how beautiful sunrises and sunsets could be seen from a spot pretty close to the Hicks mausoleum at the cemetery in Copperhill, the history of the Company copper mine, and what I knew about the doctor and the Hicks Clinic.

She listened and let me introduce her to the history, the people, and the need. A couple of times, she closed her eyes to take it all in like I have done over and over. Chaney was no stranger to adversity. She was tough enough and more than capable of sharing our stories. So I kept going.

"Tell me when you've had enough of the history. There's a tremendous amount of info to this story." I smiled, wanting her to know I understood it to be mainly dark and difficult to fathom. Ours is a tough story to hear for the first time. I told her about Kitty and the abuse she endured and about Carlynn and the gold sandals. And then I told her about a birth mother I'd met from one of the neighboring towns. I gave her Judy's story as she had told it to me.

JUDY

Neighbors were mindful of any day Judy didn't put her wares out or move them around because she rarely missed the opportunity to sell even the smallest item. The extra money earned in her front yard helped her afford what her jobs as cook and maid could not. She took donations of clothing and gave some too, depending on how threadbare her patrons were when they arrived in her yard looking for shoes or clothes or the occasional pot or pan.

Sam from down the street would come up and help himself to a coat in the winter and voluntarily relinquish it at the start of spring every year. Judy didn't mind and kept the coat off to the back of things, overseeing it through the summer to make sure it would still be there for Sam in the winter.

Occasionally, she would make repairs to the coat, stitching rips from the spills he frequently took on his walks back from Harbucks, the roadside bar locals called a gathering place. Judy would stand on her porch arching one eyebrow and give a quick huff when Sam brought eggs to her door on Monday mornings to show his appreciation for her kindness. He was always too hungover to bring the eggs over the weekend. She would take the offering and thank him as though she had concluded business at the Piggly Wiggly store, though the cashier at the store was reliably more sober. She didn't like drunks, but she never turned someone in need away.

Judy was famous for her outside yard store, and the local government even tried to have her fill out business paperwork and pay for a permit to sell. But she sweet-talked her way out of it.

She once caught two young thieves, one in each hand, with their feet dangling above the dirt. She lectured them in a low, stern manner that would scare most men. "You boys need to learn your boundaries. Can't just come up on my place and take what you want."

––––––––––––

The next day, Judy was up before the sun, trying to get her little ones ready for school and out the door before she headed to Copperhill to make a little money cooking and cleaning for Doc Hicks and his wife, Chass. Judy was also known around town for her biscuits and gravy. Everyone knew she liked to cook. It was much easier on her back than doing heavy lifting and moving, although she would do that if the opportunity came up to keep cash in the little shoebox under her bed. That shoebox kept her a few months ahead of the bill collectors. Its contents kept the lights on, and she did almost anything to fill it up.

She caught a ride into Copperhill with a neighbor and was dropped off at the bottom of the road, just below the town hall. She walked up the hill and across the railroad tracks to the Hicks house, knocked on the side door, and went into the kitchen, just how she always made her entry. The oven was waiting to be fired up and masterfully steered into producing the perfect biscuits and cinnamon buns. The house would soon be filled with the smell of sweetness. She started to unpack her bag when she heard Doc Hicks in the other room.

"Is that you, Judy?" he called.

"Yes, sir, Doc Hicks. I just came in and am starting the oven up."

"That's good, Judy. I have a few other things for you to do today as well. I'll give you a little extra. Chass isn't feeling well, and we need some laundry and cleaning done."

"Yes, sir. I'll get to it." And with that she started the biscuits and the dough for the cinnamon rolls. Once that was done, she turned her attention to getting the laundry started and scrubbing some floors. An hour after she had started the laundry, Doc Hicks called her into his office.

"Before you leave today, I'd like you to sweep and clean the floors in here too. That hasn't been done for a while."

"Yes, sir. I'll get to it as quickly as I can." Judy thought of how little time she had to get everything done.

After giving some instructions, Hicks didn't leave for the clinic but lingered at the house instead. When she couldn't put it off any longer, Judy started sweeping the floors in his office as he sat there. At first he pretended to shuffle papers and read some circulars. But as she started to clean the floors on her hands and knees, he appeared to be watching her intently. He stood up at one point and asked if she needed help with the bucket, coming closer to hover over her. When she shook her head no, he sat back down and talked about his special friends in town and how he took good care of them. And she was special too, wasn't she?

She finished the floor and with his last proposition, Judy stood in front of him and gave him the what for.

She'd been through enough in life. She had been abused, abandoned, threatened with death, disregarded, harassed by those who had husbands, and treated like the Monday morning trash. A woman shouldn't have to take this from anyone, but this was her world.

———

Chaney understood what it was for a woman to put up with adversity. She had weathered a few bumps in the road, times when she didn't fit in and was down and out. As I relayed some stories, she nodded and spoke. "I can't imagine there were many choices for women here," she said. "It's sad. I want to convey how hard it was for these women to give up a baby. How it hurt them, how they struggled."

I agreed with her. "I want the truth." As we talked, we agreed on many points and discussed the main topics to include in the *Taken at Birth* documentary—the abortions, the induced labor to meet the doctor's schedule, the risk of preemie babies, stolen babies, adults looking for the families they were stolen from, secrets kept by good old boys and nurses alike. The list was long. So long we knew it would be hard to hit just the high points, much less fit everything in. Chaney had her work cut out for her. But at the end of our conversation, she was still smiling, undaunted but weary from all the information to process.

In the same fashion Frank and my other sources told me stories, I shared what I knew with Chaney. "Paul Reymann met Judy. Carlynn introduced him to her. The three of us went over and had lunch at her house one day. He fell in love with her over a sandwich and a Coke. He thought she was his birth mother. Carlynn had to break the truth to him gently. She wasn't his birth mother." I sighed. "He laughs about it now, but he really wanted her to be his. We have all grasped at the answers."

I took a deep breath before asking, "Ready for more? It gets darker." And when she nodded, I went on.

The story of Hicks's son Walter and the mystery surrounding his death is a lingering and disgusting low point that still makes me shake my head. When I first heard it, my thoughts went to the chaos and swarm of darkness surrounding Doc Hicks and the strides he took to keep things under control. I'd heard the story several times, whispered to me like another dirty secret. In turn, I relayed it to Carlynn and later I told the dark story to Chaney. The details I'd been told years earlier poured out, and it was as though I was back in the Hickses' Tennessee home, seeing the worn hardwood floors, the faded papered walls, and the stairway to the upstairs once again. I thought of how Walter Lynn Hicks was a boy who grew up in the shadow of his father. How the night he died was shrouded in desperation and drama that surpassed the horror of his service in World War II, winding down the last moments of his life. It's a story of how a little boy looks at his father, even when he's grown.

WALTER

The word *doctor* was perfectly centered in black letters on the frosted glass door. Hicks's grown son stood mesmerized with his hand touching the doorknob. He stood there as if he had never seen it before and hesitated before pushing harder against the weight of the door, just enough to step inside. It opened and the smell of rubbing alcohol and wet towels hit him when he entered the empty room. Three days of storms had provided enough dampness to permeate the air, and the absence of sun-light added heavily to the dank smell.

Walter looked around the room for any sign of his father's presence or a sign that he might return soon. "Daddy?" he whispered. Quiet and stillness bounced back from the walls, answering him with nothing.

Rain continued to pelt the windows as thunder crashed in the distance. He closed the door behind him and looked around, this time more thoroughly. The familiar placement of the furniture reminded Walter of earlier years, growing up with a doctor for a father. The office looked the same as it had during his childhood. There was a table in the middle of the room for examining patients. Two chairs and a desk sat off to the side for consultations and paperwork when the job was done. A glass-enclosed shelf hung above a counter. Leather and stained pine, porcelain and stainless steel. He stood there in the quiet of his father's office in the Tennessee house.

Walter was the middle child of three siblings and certainly the most wayward. He was a World War II veteran and a doctor himself, having followed his father's path, at least in vocation. His older brother, Tommie Jr., was a dentist in Atlanta, and his younger sister, Margaret, was married off to a doctor. She was in Chattanooga raising a family. He had heard there were other brothers and sisters but didn't know for sure, not having seen them himself. The McCaysville grapevine spoke of a brother who looked just like him, only with brighter red hair, but those were only rumors. Everyone knew that his father always prided himself on keeping busy. That is, keeping busy in this room and with the ladies in town. And he heard the unknown brother was a doctor too, with his education paid for by Thomas Jugarthy Hicks himself.

Walter's hands moved slowly, touching the fixtures and surfaces, taking the cold hardness in through his fingers and his thoughts. The angles and peaks pressed against his fingertips, catching every so often where the years had roughed the wood or chipped the porcelain. His eyes followed and explored like a sponge, processing the part they played in the day-to-day doctoral business.

A flash of lightning caught his eye and swung him around to the windowed side of the room where his father's desk and over-stuffed leather chair sat. A few scuff marks charted the chair's movement over the decades. The leather still smelled of musk. The softness was almost too much to bear in the midst of all the memories and emotions running through his head.

Walter sank into the chair and thought for some time about the conflict that had filled this room over the years: the push and pull of life and death, the dance of what to do, and the relationship between himself and his father. Rain now drummed the windows with a slow, steady pace. Now it hit more like an assault, sheeting the glass and streaming down to the already-soaked earth. The sound comforted Walter, lulling him into a memory from years ago, the first time he snuck into his father's office.

———————

"Son, what are you doing in here?" His father's face pulled tight, eyes flaring, as he glanced at his young son who was standing on a chair in the breached office.

The fierce concern in the doctor's voice scared Walter, stifling any response to cover up what he was doing. The chair was still pushed up to the counter next to the porcelain sink basin, and Walter's heart rate picked up the pace as he saw the bloody stainless steel pan, his whole body struggling and at a loss of speech. "Nothing, I swear, Daddy! I didn't touch nothin', swear!"

Guilty eyes stuck to the counter, giving him up. His body still trembling and shaking from the surprise scrutiny of being found in the office in the first place, he couldn't take his eyes away for more than one blink and he knew he was in trouble. He had entered a forbidden place. Warned to never go into the office unless his father was with him, he knew better than to push him. This was a breach not to be forgiven or forgotten anytime soon, and as the needy, middle child, he would pay dearly in scrutiny going forward.

Doctor Hicks stood in the doorway, motionless, staring at the boy. A few moments later, he spoke in a deliberate, low tone, forcing Walter's attention. "Why are the blinds open?"

Again, silence. "Did you hear me, child?" And then, "Walter?" Hicks took a step forward, shut the door behind him, and turned the key. Softer and gentler, he repeated his question. "Did you hear me? Why are the blinds open?"

Walter stared at his father, refusing to answer in fear.

Hicks directed him, "Sit down where you are. Don't move until I'm done, you hear me?"

Walter stiffly nodded his head in agreement and got off the chair and sat on the wood floor next to the examining table. Its sheet straps brushed his back and neck as he lowered himself slowly to the floor, trying to keep from crying. He whimpered as he concentrated on what his father was doing.

The doctor turned to Walter and started to speak but stopped short when his eyes drifted above his son to the examination table where a huddle of sheets rested. "I'll be just a minute. Don't move until I tell you."

Again, Walter agreed and sat still. He knew being a doctor was important, and he wanted to be one too. He sat silently, intent on learning from his father's actions. Doc Hicks halfway glanced to the wide-eyed child sitting on the floor.

He worked to clean up from a previous appointment. He wrestled with one of the stainless pans, spilling and splashing the contents onto the floor. Walter, still striving to concentrate and be a good little doctor, did not notice the splashing right away.

Moisture formed at the back of his neck, tickling and tempting movement, he dared move his hand to wipe it away. Pulling it back from his neck, red liquid that was thick like paint stained his fingertips and was smeared across his palm. Horror forced words from his mouth that he could not find before, and in a panic, he let loose everything that he should have said and done. He spoke in between gulps of air and tears. "I just wanted to see what was in here, Daddy! That's all! That's all I wanted, honest. The blinds were shut, and I opened them just cuz I wanted to see. I did not touch nothin', honest."

He held out his palm, panicked and close to howling. "Daddy! Look, I'm bleeding!"

His backside was still planted firmly against the floor when his father calmly walked toward him, bending down with the rag to wipe away the smattering of blood on the boy's neck and hair. Walter didn't know what to expect or where the blood came from. All the drama poured from him in an instant. Doc Hicks threw the bloody rag into a pan and motioned him to stand. He did so, still trembling as his father quietly and tenderly instructed young Walter what to do in the future when his curiosity got the best of him.

———————————

Walter was comfortable in the chair as the memory of his childhood came to an end. He thought of his life and all the mistakes he had made, the abrupt turns and direct, reckless decisions. Looking back, he could see some of it was inherited: drug use to numb the pain, womanizing, blurring lines, and trying to fix it all and climb up from the bottom. Some of it was pain from his time in the war, the shock from witnessing so much death and dying. After a few more moments, he decided it was time to go upstairs to his room, the one his mother had kept for him in this house he grew up in. He made it to the top of the steps and into the room and climbed into bed, capping the night off with a morphine mix of sleeping drugs Daddy provided to settle him down from the nightmares of the war. He fell into sleep soon after.

His eyes abruptly opened to the shotgun resting against his skin, sending vibrations from his father's shaking hand across the metal and into the muscles of his chest. Sweat dropped into his eyes as he tried to focus on the face and make sense of the predicament where he now found himself firmly placed. He could smell the fresh flowers sitting on the side table and the starched linens his mother's housekeeper put on the bed that morning, even through the dampness the thunderstorms put into the air. Lightning lit up the night and electricity surged, bringing his full attention to the man who stood above him, staring and silent, leaving him stunned in fear and confusion. The morphine still pounded at his head and kept him in slow motion, numbing him from the pain of the bullet that ripped through him. His body slumped. His eyes met his father's one last time before they closed. His father had stumbled backward with the jolt. Thunder rolled in the background as Doc Hicks laid the gun in his son's hands and wiped the splattering of blood off his own cheeks with his handkerchief.

I met Chaney's eyes and continued, "That's the story I've heard a few times over the years. One of my sources was one of the first on the scene. The authorities told everyone it was a suicide, but that's not how it seemed to the ones who were there to get the body and all. The shotgun was too long for Walter's arms. That was 1967. His mother died a couple years later, and then Hicks died in 1972. I found a tiny article years ago referring to a robbery at the Hicks house. It said the doctor and his wife were tied up and Hicks beaten. Oh, and one of my sources said some of his fingernails were taken off. They said it was Walter looking for money or drugs. Not sure we'll ever really know the truth."

Chaney had the same look on her face that I imagined I bore when first hearing these details. Years ago I just shook my head, but now the story makes me cry. No one can water down Walter's alleged suicide or explain the facts away. The odds of successfully using a shotgun, which is longer than your arms, to kill yourself are pretty slim. A glaring, inconvenient truth.

I told story after story and those helped form a rough draft for the direction of the docuseries. And as with an old wooden roller coaster, Chaney and I pulled the safety bar down across our laps, felt the chain on the tracks pull and take hold of the cart, clanking and jerking and slapping the wooden slats as it rolled over them. With the sun and wind in our faces, the coaster sped up as much as it could to take us up to the top, and with steeled hearts and minds, we prepared for the drop.

SIXTEEN

Taken at Birth—
Time Well Spent

W E ALL FELT LIKE STARS while filming, if only for a few moments. Here we were gathered again, Hicks Babies coming together as a group to share our story. We had leaned on each other at times and then stayed away from each other at other times. Being a Hicks Baby can be tricky. The group filmed mostly in Georgia and Tennessee. It was a good opportunity for everyone to visit our roots, some for the first time. The production of the docuseries felt like a mix of herding cats and primping to make sure we looked nice on camera. We all had a good time filming. The cameras made for a good distraction from the burden of our mission to find the truth. Chaney and her crew had to put up with all of us. Although we crowned her a Hicks Clinic Alumni—a title given to those permanently connected to us through the Hicks Clinic—Chaney still had the daunting task of putting our story out there for the world to see.

We planned to shoot some of *Taken at Birth* at TLC's studio in LA, so soon after filming in Georgia, I was on my way west. When I arrived, Chaney was there to meet me, and she wanted to talk about that day's shoot.

"The subject matter expert, the doctor specializing in preemies, is here already; he's been here for a while and we've chatted a little. Wait until you hear what he has to say. I think you'll find what you've been looking for."

I nodded. TLC was holding up their end of the bargain. They promised to give me support in further investigating things I hadn't been able to discover over the years for lack of resources and time. We sought out expertise in the neonatal field to confirm our theory that many of the babies sold by Hicks had been preemies. The studio was helping connect the pieces I had wanted to find over the years, and those pieces were finally coming together.

The preemie doctor was poised and mild-mannered but nerdy in a good way. We introduced ourselves and discussed the story of the Hicks Clinic and progressed to the likelihood of preemies being born there. So many of us were tiny with low birth weights and health issues commonly found in premature births. It was good to find expert data to support what we had thought all along. But when the doctor began to explain the details of the process of induction—the risks and the projected percentage of survival—reality hit home.

He estimated the survival rate for this risky procedure was 50 percent at best. He might as well have hit me with a baseball bat. So many lives were endangered all because Doc Hicks had a customer waiting to buy a baby. I thought of those babies, the half that didn't have a chance. I was one of the survivors, and it was overwhelming to think of all the ones who didn't make it out of the clinic.

The stories of Doc Hicks storing babies in jars at different stages of development and the rumors of how he had paraded one out when he needed some sort of evidence after being questioned about a baby dying screamed into my mind. He had to show proof when he got pushback. And there were even stories of him throwing babies into the river. That seems laughable until you think of everything else that took place at the clinic. When you consider that rumor on a corporate level, you almost believe it. There are no graves for them, nothing to acknowledge these lost lives. Nothing.

Producing the docuseries brought up many memories from my past I thought were lost or reconciled. Filming in and around McCaysville and Copperhill would sometimes stop me in my tracks, startled by a memory as it materialized in front of me like a ghost. Memories of years of looking at those buildings and streets, pushing myself to understand their importance. If only they could open wide and tell me the stories I suspected and the truth I longed to know.

Where did the women who left the clinic with empty arms and no baby to hold go for healing? Where did the women found bleeding and butchered on the curb in front of the clinic end up? Did they make it? And who put comforting arms around them and assured them they weren't alone? That they were worth love and care? It was emotional and exhausting at times, yet also cathartic.

One particular day, while the cameras followed us as we walked and talked, I looked up at one of the brick buildings on the main street. It was once the busiest and most distinct hotel in town. And it reminded me of the story of a birth mother who had lost hope.

DOTTIE

She was pretty in a clean, classic way. Not a knockout beauty like Sophia Loren or Raquel Welch. She was more like Grace Kelly or Audrey Hepburn. Her entrance into McCaysville and Copperhill wasn't heralded by bands playing or signs welcoming and proclaiming anything out of the ordinary. Dorothy, or Dottie to most, had returned to the small town she had visited a couple years prior. She paid for her stay at the hotel and made her way to the room she requested: the one on the corner, overlooking the street toward the McCaysville side. The small, sparse room with a thin chenille bedspread folded at the bottom of the bed and perfectly starched sheets that she ran her hands over was only a short-term distraction. She had come here to look for something she had lost, and yet at the same time, she knew it couldn't be found. Her first visit to town was seven years before. She had made several trips up from Atlanta, but she hadn't been back for almost two years.

Those two years passed slowly, and making a trip back to McCaysville and the Hicks Clinic had become an obsession for Dottie. She slipped away to the North Georgia town every time her husband was on a business trip. The housekeeper suspected a liaison but never said anything, quietly assisting with her bags, helping her pack the car for the drive, and closing up the house for a few days.

The memory and heartbreak of the night Dottie gave birth and the baby girl she gave up had almost killed her. The physical pain was no comparison to the pain of having her baby taken out of her arms. She couldn't escape the hurt but had come here to try and get lost, to attempt to stop the pain of her memories. She sat in the old chair by the window, still in the clothes she drove up in, and watched the street until the sun had gone down and everything slowed to a stop. And she sat there all night watching the shadows until the sun came back into view in the morning. Noises from the hallway got her attention and jolted her out of the chair. Stumbling and falling into the bed, she slept. She was exhausted.

The sun was bright and straight up in the sky when she woke after the needed sleep. Her eyes open and acclimating to the room, she cried over the misery of being in the town again. Hungry and still in the crumpled, day-old clothes, she got up, bathed, fixed her hair, and dressed so she could get something to eat. The diner would do just fine, and she headed there and found a seat by the window. After she ordered lunch, she contemplated why and how she had so often been drawn to visit the one place that brought so many sleepless and disjointed nights. Her baby was beautiful with dark hair and olive skin, perfect fingers and toes. Her baby, the baby she had wanted her entire life. She would be almost seven now. The father was a college affair during her senior year. He was dark and handsome. She had thought they would marry until her family drew the line between her and the man. He was from the wrong side of town and poor by their standards; he wouldn't do. The decision to give the baby to some other woman was made quickly. Dottie graduated and stayed out of sight until it was time. And then she was sent off to the North Georgia town of McCaysville. She married a solid, respectable man two years after the birth. She had everything she needed and most of what she wanted. Her life was a societal dream of beautiful houses, clothes, jewelry, traveling, and propriety. Her marriage was safe but childless. There was no hope of another baby, and she was feeling the void more than ever. Her life had reached a tipping point.

Back in the diner, she paid for her meal and walked down the street to the Hicks Clinic that used to bustle with activity. The building was empty now and no one even looked at it. It sat there, just a shell of what it once was. She had no one to ask where her baby went or where she could find her. She was suddenly tired and returned to the hotel, once again sitting at the window looking out. Late into the evening she poured a glass of water and reached for her bag, several bottles of pills spilling out across the floor as she did. She stared at them, lost in her plan for this trip, her intended last visit to the Hicks Clinic. The pills were enough to just close her eyes and go to sleep and not open them again. She had enough but could wait one more night, so she scooped them all up and shoved them back into the bag. She shuddered at the thought of what the bag held and began crying again before she fell asleep. Her tears brought dreams of a baby girl and her pleading for God to help her find peace. She dreamed of soft blue and pink cotton candy clouds.

The next morning brought more sunshine and her stomach lurched. She felt an urgency to get out of the room as quickly as she could. She dressed, left the hotel, and found herself walking toward the clinic once again. She looked at the building and slowly shook away the memories of the sterile rooms, the mixed smell of detergents and medicines, and the bed. The hard, tightly sheeted and squeaky bed. She almost fell to the ground just outside the building. It was hot out and she hadn't eaten or drunk anything yet and she felt her head swimming. She stuck out like the outsider she was, dressed in expensive, high-fashion clothing and delicately made slip-ons, the look you would see at Buckhead in Atlanta, not McCaysville or Copperhill. Her blonde hair was slicked back and smooth, sunglasses covered her swollen eyes, head down and bobbing slowly. She was sobbing now.

She was lost in the moment and didn't care about anything until she heard a little girl's voice. "Mama, why is she crying? Is she hurt?" Dottie pulled her shoulders back and looked around, honing in on the voice. It came from a little girl about five or six, who was holding the hand of a pretty and proper lady. They were about ten feet away and looking at her worriedly.

"Do you mind if we come closer? Are you all right?" The deep Southern drawl poured into Dottie's ears like a fancy white linen dinner invitation with gold edging and embossed black letters announcing a special event. Again, the woman asked, "Can we come closer?"

Dottie found her voice in time, though a bit shaken, and told them she was all right. She said she was just hungry and not feeling too well, then she told them they could come closer. She was conscious of the mascara running down her face and her smeared lipstick but couldn't do much to fix either. The pretty lady offered her a kerchief. Before long, the two were chatting away about dresses and recipes. And the dark-haired little girl was entranced by the intricate details of Dottie's blonde hair, diamond ring, and uptown way.

They all walked together to the diner and continued the conversation, smiling and laughing as they shared so much. It was as though they had known each other all their lives, and Dottie found some peace as she drank her iced tea and picked at the sandwich on her plate. The pretty lady smiled at her and asked Dottie what she was doing in McCaysville, noting the absence of an accent like hers.

Dottie stopped everything and lost her poker face. Showing all of her cards, she confessed, "I was at the clinic once." Her eyes welled again, and she turned away to get it together, trying not to let the little girl see her face. Dottie continued very quietly, "She'd be seven. I gave her up seven years ago. And I can't bear . . ." She trailed off before finishing the sentence, and the women's eyes met, one's filled with pain and the other's under-standing and empathetic.

In a way only a child can, the little girl lightened the moment. She started singing a bouncy kind of song about sunshine, lol-lipops, and flowers. It was a silly song with a good rhythm. Both the women laughed and began to sing with her, joining in as children themselves.

When things settled down at the table, the mother looked at Dottie, smiling, and said, "God doesn't want you to hurt. He wants you to live your life. You've done nothing wrong. God loves you. Live every day, not just yesterday." With that, Dottie was brought to tears again and thanked the near-stranger. They said goodbye as Dottie held her arms wide open and hugged them both so it was understood how much that afternoon had meant to her. Two strangers and a small child, one close in age to Dot-tie's lost little girl. That day had set an unanticipated movement of forgiveness into motion. Dottie knew she would never see these two again, and she couldn't explain to her husband how she knew them or what secret had been shared, but she was so grateful for their shared moments.

Back in her hotel room, Dottie lay across the bed sideways and slept once more, waking several hours later to darkness. Once she got her bearings, she reached for the bag with the pills that rattled like a snake in the bottom of the bag. She had come here with a purpose, to end the pain of losing her little girl, and for the first time, she fought against that misguided relief. Then, like a recording, she heard the voice of the little girl singing of sunshine and flowers. The memory permeated her mind and she heard herself laughing. Suddenly she was no longer in such desperate pain. The pills found their way to the toilet, and Dottie sat in the chair and looked out again. This time she thought of the future and living life, forgiven and hopeful.

"She wasn't the only one to come back looking for her baby, but she was the only one who said she wanted to die," I said as I finished telling Dottie's story. "She went on to live a good life. She had children later but didn't feel she could tell her secret or find her baby girl. To me, that's the saddest part of the Hicks Clinic tragedies—too many secrets."

Chaney nodded. "It's too many."

Unloading twenty-plus years of assessing what had been done and how it could have been different if I had made other decisions with my search was freeing. The docuseries brought an opportunity to mend some fences and embrace new perspectives on the past. I wished Michelle was there to share in the bounty of closure with the story.

There was a lot of tying of loose ends for me and the experience was good and welcome. We wrapped up the last week of filming back in McCaysville, and Chaney and I found ourselves at the Blue Ridge Inn, reminiscing over the almost two years of production from scripting and filming the whole way to the show's premiere. We laughed about the predicaments she and her crew had faced and shook our heads at the hurdles that, most of the time, appeared out of nowhere. Chaney had done her job but also made a personal connection to this story, investing in those from the Hicks Clinic.

We sat in the parlor of the inn one last time and relaxed. It had been a long endeavor. We talked about everything she and her crew had done to make it work and then discussed what was left and how, after all the years of searching and uncovering, I still had my work cut out for me. There were still many leads to run and so many more stories to uncover. Just like at the beginning of the search, I had work to do. I hadn't fully uncovered the part the late Reid Brown played in the Hicks Clinic. He was the doctor who grew up in Isabella, the tiny town close to McCaysville. He was the doctor who eventually became Doc Hicks's son-in-law and a possible connection to Chattanooga and more babies. There were still Hicks Babies in need of birth family information. Paul Reymann's birth story had recently been discovered and had so many twists and turns that needed to be scrutinized. Michelle's father was out there somewhere. And I needed to find Kitty's babies.

Chaney and I talked about all the leads from 1997 and the ways they crossed over into some of those we found during the filming process. She leaned back into her chair and asked a final, semiofficial question. "After all this and revisiting your journey, after all the years of tracking this story down, after everything you know of him, how do you feel about Doctor Hicks?"

SEVENTEEN

Finding Home

A MILLION TIMES. I have heard that question a million times. *How do you feel about Doctor Hicks?* That time it hit me differently. Because of the rehashing of events during filming, scrutinizing the Hicks Clinic and Doc Hicks, it was cutting when Chaney asked for my opinion on the man. The baby seller, the scoundrel, the father, the town doctor. The man was heralded as a saving grace by some and a demon by others. Hearing the stories and firsthand accounts had stirred up anger in me at times and at other times, pity and disappointment.

Over the years, I've struggled with his life but know that mine has been less than angelic. I've broken rules and stumbled on my path and sometimes caused others to stumble. I've been granted grace, but judgment is too easy to make of others. Judgment is the path of least resistance. This man was just that, a man. By telling one last story of Doc Hicks, I felt we could close this day out.

THOMAS JUGARTHY HICKS

He was sitting in the back of the church, in the last pew, the one next to the sanctuary doors. He dared not go in farther, go any closer to the pulpit where the congregation would see too much of him. The choir took its place behind the pastor and began singing about grace and love. The pastor turned and signaled the dutiful Sunday morning worshipers to join them in a song. Voices rose to the Almighty in a small roar as the people of McCaysville gave their all. The beauty of the words and sounds made him feel all right while he sat there, like he was almost a part of something clean and smooth. A quiet observer, he didn't want to be heard any more than he wanted to be seen. He closed his eyes. There were no smells of alcohol swabs or endless questions from patients, only the sweet sound of forgiveness and peace. He stayed there as long as he could.

———

With a stir from somewhere in the back of the room, Doc Hicks opened his eyes but not to the peacefulness and loving hymns of the church from years in the past. He wasn't in the church at the moment. He looked around to gather his bearings and reality brought him back to the present quickly. It was the fall of 1964, and he was on trial. He sat next to his lawyer near a jury box of his peers in the Fannin County Courthouse. Old and frail from leukemia, he still had that grin on his face, as though it could never be erased. His peers, Fannin County residents, were now sitting in judgment of something no one wanted to be a part of, much less admit to knowing about. The small group of men included some who had witnessed the good old days of Doc Hicks hopping down the streets of Copperhill and McCaysville on a pogo stick without a care in the world or driving the streets in his fancy car. Pity was on their minds as they looked at him now. No one wanted to be where he sat. Not one of them.

Some of the men nodded, business partners of sorts or his coconspirators who were hoping to go unnoticed but acted cordially toward him at the same time. Some had seen him slip into the back of the church sanctuary on a Sunday morning and had wondered what he was doing there. The good old boys and good old days somehow came together in that courtroom like a pair of cymbals in a loud, metallic jolt. And there they were, watching the late stages of decline of a man's body and possibly his soul. And that's what they did. They watched. They all knew, or at least assumed, he was guilty, and some but not all of them were guilty right alongside him, as they had fathered a baby and needed his assistance a time or two. They knew about the abortions and the baby selling as well. Someone had had enough of the cruelty and turned him in with enough fervor to force a corrupt system to face Thomas J. Hicks, his swindling, and his lies. Birds of a feather, they say. The trial was practically a holiday for those outside of the good old boy circle in McCaysville, Georgia.

I finished the story and turned to Chaney. "I don't judge Hicks anymore."

Chaney showed no surprise; she knew what I meant. She didn't have to say a word because she understood this journey. We left it at that and said goodbye. Chaney had a plane to catch back to Los Angeles, and I yearned for the sunset at the cemetery.

Judgment is a dirty word. I've sat in the back of a few churches a time or two myself, trying to hide. I thank God I've never been in a courtroom sitting next to a jury box with my peers scrutinizing my life and rendering judgment.

As I sat down on the cemetery lawn, I considered how thankful I was for the journey that brought me to this place under the sun and stars. The grass under my quilt smelled good and sweet from a fresh mowing, and I settled in for another beautiful sunset and thought about judging Doc Hicks and the way his life entwined with mine all these years. I thought about the way things had changed from my birth to the first time I danced on his grave and how all the events of my life had brought me here: from my childhood of hearing about stolen babies and what that meant for my family to searching for clues of the Hicks Clinic and, finally, to finding who I am. And again, in a step back in time, I closed my eyes and gave up the censoring that protected like a wall around my heart and settled into truth, looking at the impact the search had upon my life.

Everything that had happened in 1997 hit me at once, and I wasn't prepared. Looking back on it, my spiritual walk was what surprised me most. I found God when I was twenty-one, dropping to my knees and asking Him to show me who He was. He answered and I followed. But in 1997, when I was thirty-two, what I thought was solid and could withstand whatever came my way crumbled. I was overwhelmed and walked away from everything: my friends, my marriage, and my relationship with God. I was drowning and would come up every so often to take a breath and see what damage I was doing. And then I made the decision to just go away and live the life I wanted with no one to tell me what to do or that I was less than. There was too much going on in my head. A battle between peace and turmoil was taking place.

I wanted to erase everything, everyone, and every point of contention or disappointment in my life. And then I let loose of God too. I packed my bags and left, and for fifteen years, outside of time spent with Carlynn and John, I wandered around broken and alone, searching for fulfillment in shallow, physical, and material things and hoping to fill the void I had willfully and knowingly created for myself when I walked away. I left everything behind to find who I was and where I belonged. Those fifteen years just about broke me, and I defiantly ignored God's voice until several successive life events brought me to my knees once again, and I set my hope on God and rededicated my life to Him. He saw this prodigal and stood at the gate of the yard, watching down the road as I neared, and He welcomed me back with overwhelming love. He was faithful even though I hadn't been. And mercifully, I'd come full circle. I had finally come home.

All these years later, after finding my birth story and my way back to God, I find myself again sitting in the grass at the cemetery with the quilt wrapped around me and looking out at the hills, taking it all in for the thousandth time. Just a-ways over my shoulder sits the Hicks mausoleum and I can say now that I know who Thomas Jugarthy Hicks was. Just a man. He was a human being just like me. And he was a mess. I'm a mess. I no longer have a desire to judge him. I no longer need to dance on his grave. My heart is full and I can laugh and cry as memories of my embarrassments, missteps, and victories parade through my mind while the sun slowly moves away. And I can hear the many voices of the women telling their stories to me, and I can see the babies they spoke of and I can feel the desperation. The sounds, smells, and all of the fight-or-flight moments from the years of searching wash over me and I can't sit any longer. So I stand and raise my hands in thankfulness and reverence to the One who knew me all along.

Conclusion

And Love Is Everything

A COUPLE TIMES A YEAR I make my way back down south and stand on the invisible line between Copperhill and McCaysville, looking at them like it's the first time I've set eyes on the two small towns that are connected at the hip like conjoined twins. Sometimes it hurts to think of the beginning of my search and the challenges I faced over the years to get to where I am today. How I wanted it to be simple, for the answers to come easy, for there to be no prejudice and no resistance. I hurt, wishing I knew then what I know now and how much could've been avoided if I had known. The perfectionist in me mourns over the sometimes-awkward imperfection of my journey. If I had it to do over again, I'd drive into McCaysville and walk right into that small diner and ask all the right questions, make all the right moves, and eat my breakfast without worry. I'd roll that town up and put it in my pocket as though it were mine.

Now, I see the town for what it is—a place where imperfect people live and love and strive to protect what's theirs.

Generations have passed and cleared out the goings-on of the Hicks Clinic and those who enabled its doctor to do so much damage. All of the looking away and not saying anything is gone. The town has had several face-lifts since that time. New buildings, facades, businesses, and finally, an upright police department and a lot of transplants from Atlanta, Asheville, and the surrounding states to replace the scourge of fiefdoms, the hypocrisy, and the corruption of the old ways. I see it as beautiful now, more beautiful than I could ever have imagined it in the beginning. And on some days, I believe it embraces me.

Even with all of the newness and revitalized life in McCaysville, in my mind's eye, I can still see birth mothers shuffling around, struggling with their shame and trying to blend in. Like an old black-and-white movie starting to spin on the reel, through a fuzzy lens the fifties and sixties slowly return to the town and I strain to see the faces of the women walking around, working in the hair salon or cleaning off tables at one of the restaurants. In my memories, I can still see my face in the glass of the windows of the downtown stores, with my back turned to the street, watching everyone passing by in the reflection and studying them for some clue or sign. With everything in my being, I had hoped they belonged to me. Then I shake my thoughts enough to break the connection to those early days of searching. And I take a deep breath.

My birth mother never showed up to meet me as I had hoped she would, but I discovered an understanding and a love for her on those streets. I learned some of my own lessons in unconditional love there. I found what was more important than a birth mother and more satisfying than all the answers I sought. I found where I belonged. It took the journey of searching, not the actual DNA, to find who I am. I'm a child of God. He knows my name and He placed me in this world. He knew where I should be and who I belonged to all along. I'm His.

And I'm Herbert's girl. I have no doubt that I'm the daughter of a good man. I can clearly see his love and exuberance for life through the stories given to me by my cousins and his other children. He worked hard and played hard as he danced his way through life and touched everyone with his smile. I see him as a young man in the old and faded black-and-white pictures from World War II, standing in his uniform. And I'm proud to be his. I'm the sister of motorcycle-riding, rebellious, and wonderful Tommy, and because of him, I now have a niece who sings like a beautiful sunrise, praising God and proclaiming His love and forgiveness. Cousins Donna and Jeannie know. I'm a Cruce. I'm Grandma Maude Estelle Cruce's grandbaby. This I'm sure of, and no one can take that away from me now.

I'm from the Hunnicut line, and my maternal great-grand-father and great-great-grandfather were preachers who loved God. Protection and faith were handed down to me through the generations because I'm theirs. They were tall and thin, farm-ers on the days around Sunday, and I belong to them. I'm the granddaughter of a woman more than familiar with moonshine and bootlegging, and I chuckle at the thought. My heart covets the stories of her adventures, and I yearn to have heard her voice telling them. I belong to my twin uncles, William and Wesley, and my great-aunt Betty, uncle Harve, and cousins Amy and Lisa, Opal and Joe. No one can deny me anymore. They are my kindred spirits. They are mine.

I belong to fried chicken Friday nights at the base of Blalock Mountain in Turtletown and to the many years' worth of sitting on Carlynn's front porch learning about humming-birds, sweet tea, and fireflies and how loving someone doesn't make them perfect. Carlynn taught me so much but mostly she loved me and held me like a mother holds her daughter and tells her it will be all right. I had never known that before her.

I'll always be Kitty's girl because she is a part of me, and I long to reach out to her and tell her it's okay. My tapestry has her woven in it as shiny threads of gold and silver, and she will never go away from my heart. She will always shine. I belong to a pair of gold sandals as I dance with joy in my heart, the same gold sandals that brought a moment of redemption to Kitty's broken soul. I'm Charlie's girl too. He deserves to have some peace about the beauty Kitty brought to him in his youth among the wildflowers.

I belong to Jim and Joan and hold them dear and thank God that I can now forgive them and understand where the pain of my childhood and growing up came from and that it's okay. I can now hold Joan close in my heart and remember how she tried so hard and know she was as much a lost child as I was. I wish I could go back and belt out hymns with Elvis as I sweep the floor to the scratchy beat of the old vinyl album on the turntable at the house on Belden Avenue in Akron. I belong to my beautiful redheaded sister, Michelle, my cousin David, and the Hudkins clan. Aunt Darlene and Uncle Robby, Cousins Robin, James, and Thomas. My Hicks Baby cousin, Markie, who passed before his thirteenth birthday, well before his time, his birth story stolen and then destroyed. I belong to him. And to Cousin Kyra, who loves God with all her heart and is not afraid to show it. They are all mine and I love them.

Belonging is where unconditional love is, where you want to be. Home is when, not where. It's when you accept that love is king and it's almost always imperfect. Finding home is when you reject the judgment, the hate, and the shame, and you embrace the laughter, the frailty, the dance, and ultimately the love.

And love is everything.

Acknowledgments

THIS JOURNEY HAS been a lifetime in the making, and wonderful souls have nurtured me along the way. To them, I'm forever grateful.

The good people of McCaysville and Copperhill who have watched me peek in windows and doorways, make hopeful small talk with them, and sometimes make a little noise. To them, I say thank you for putting up with me and the Hicks Clinic story.

A heartfelt thank-you to Sharlene Martin of Martin Literary Management, who has partnered with me through this process and has tirelessly worked to bring this story to the world with her wisdom, expertise, and professionalism.

I'm honored to have been chosen by Revell to represent them with my story and am forever indebted to the Revell team for their expertise and support.

This journey would never have made its way to the pages without Revell Senior Editor Vicki Crumpton. To describe her dedication and patience would easily overtake every inch of this page, so I will simply say she is wonderful.

And finally, to the One who has known all along who I am and has loved me from the start.

Jane Blasio is a Hicks Baby, sold at birth and passed through the back door of a clinic in North Georgia. She has served for more than nineteen years in federal law enforcement. An expert in illegal adoption, she helped unravel the mystery of the Hicks Clinic, breaking the story in 1997. She has appeared on CNN, *ABC Primetime*, *Good Morning America*, Fox News, *Inside Edition*, and *Entertainment Tonight*, as well as in the *New York Times*, *People*, and *Reader's Digest*. She was the investigative lead on the recent TLC docuseries *Taken at Birth*. Jane currently lives in Akron, Ohio, and spends as much time as she can with family and friends.

CONNECT WITH JANE!

WWW.JANEBLASIO.COM